BICYCLE

HELEN PIDD

Love your bike: the complete guide to everyday cycling

PENGUIN BOOKS

CONTENTS

INTRODUCTION

'The two-wheeled velocipede is the animal which is to supersede everything else. It costs but little to produce, and still less to keep. It does not eat cart loads of hay, and does not wax fat and kick. It is easy to handle. It never rears up. It won't bite. It needs no check or rein or halter, or any unnatural restraint. It is little and light, let alone it will lean lovingly against the nearest support. It never flies off at a tangent unless badly managed and under no circumstances will it shy at anything . . .'

The Velocipedist, New York, 1 February 1869

Is there any invention more marvellous than the bicycle? When Radio 4's *You and Yours* conducted a poll in 2005 to find out what listeners considered 'the most significant technological innovation since 1800', the bicycle won almost 60 per cent of the vote, streets ahead of the computer, radio and television. It is hard to think of any other manmade object that provides joy, exercise and transport for so many people at such a low cost. When velocipedomania took hold in the late nineteenth century with the large-scale manufacture of the bicycle's forerunner, the velocipede, Victorians were agog at the capability of this 'mechanical horse'. Over in the United States in 1869, J. T. Goddard wrote with awe of 'a wonderful and fascinating little two-wheeled machine, upon which one could so gracefully annihilate time and space'.

A hundred and fifty years on, riding a bike that Goddard would easily recognize as a close relative of his own, I feel the same. Sometimes, when I'm whizzing down a hill, the wind in my hair and a daft smile on my face, I can't quite believe that a combination of metal, rubber and plastic can bring me such pleasure.

Ever since my dad unscrewed the stabilizers from my first bike and I wobbled off down our road on my own, cycling has been part of my life. When I was little, it gave me the freedom to get to the shop and buy sweets without my mum finding out; as I got older, it sped me to lectures on time when I had slept through my alarm. Nowadays, my bike gets me to work, transports my groceries, takes me on adventures and shows me new places – and I would be lost (and late) without it.

I'm not the only one. Though it hasn't yet become 'the animal . . . to supersede everything else', more and more people are rediscovering cycling as the most civilized, economic, ecological and enjoyable way of getting from A to B.

In 2009, the UK experienced its highest level of cycling for seventeen years, according to the national cyclists' organization the CTC (Cyclists' Touring Club). There are many reasons why – a hugely successful initiative from the government to provide tax-free bikes for those wanting to cycle to work, the ever-rising price in petrol and an increased awareness of environmental issues, to name but three.

But compared with countries such as Holland and Denmark, which have invested heavily in cycling infrastructure, in the UK, riding a bicycle still remains a minority activity. According to Department of Transport figures from 2007, just 1 per cent of journeys in the UK are made by bike, even though 43 per cent of people aged five and over own one. That's partially because cycling has an image problem, many people believing it to be difficult, frightening and expensive. I hope this book will convince you it isn't.

You don't need to change your life to fit in cycling. You can fit cycling into the life you have already. I'm not trying to turn you into a Serious Cyclist. You're just you, same as always, but on a bike.

I'm going to guide you through every aspect of cycling, whether you're new to the saddle or have been riding for years, by providing answers to those niggling questions you might have at the back of your mind. What's the point of buying an expensive bike? How can I avoid getting knocked off? Will anything deter a really determined bike thief? Is it worth learning how to mend a puncture when the man in the bike shop will do it for me for a tenner?

I know the answers to all these questions because I've been there. I've had three bikes stolen in three years and learned the hard way that scrimping on locks is a false economy. I've gone to work with black nails after fixing a puncture by the side of the road. I've been patronized by bike snobs, bamboozled in bike shops and searched for years to find a helmet that didn't make my head look like a cannonball. I've cycled in dresses and heels and survived Tour de France climbs as well as Britain's busiest roads. If I haven't done it myself, I've talked to police officers, campaigners, bike shop assistants, mechanics and fashion designers who have.

By the end of this book, I hope you'll be itching to go for a ride. But to start you off, here are ten of the best reasons to get on your bike:

NO CYCLING

f you cycle, you are not at the mercy of bus routes, train timetables or road-
works. A bicycle doesn't experience delays when there are leaves on the line.
t doesn't stop operating at midnight. It never runs out of petrol. It can take you
where you want, when you want, and you always know what time you'll arrive.

T WILL SAVE YOU MONEY

f I relied on public transport to travel the four miles to work and back every day,
would spend over £1,000 a year. If I drove, the bill for petrol, tax, insurance,
parking and an MOT would come to at least that amount – before I'd even
actored in the cost of buying a car. By comparison, even if I treated myself to a
swish new bike every twelve months and had it properly serviced twice yearly,
would still be saving a lot of money.

T'S A GREAT STRESS RELIEVER

Arthur Conan Doyle wrote, 'When the spirits are low, when the day appears
dark, when work becomes monotonous, when hope hardly seems worth having,
ust mount a bicycle and go out for a spin down the road, without thought on
anything but the ride you are taking.' After a bad day at the office, getting on
your bike and pounding the pedals makes everything better. If I have a tough
decision to make, I go for a ride. I always have a much clearer perspective when
'm done.

T'S SUPER EFFICIENT

As a human-powered way of getting from A to B, cycling is much less work
han running or walking, and way more fun on the downhills. You use around
20 per cent of the same energy to cycle a mile as you do to walk it.

T WILL MAKE YOU FIT

Start cycling regularly, and you'll have a healthier heart, stronger lungs, a
irmer bum and much lovelier legs. Unlike many other forms of physical

6. IT'S EMPOWERING

↘ Whether it's mending your first puncture, completing a charity bike ride or making it up a steep hill, cycling is a great confidence booster. It is also a political force for good. The suffragettes cycled, seeing the bicycle as a key tool in the emancipation of women. In the Minneapolis Tribune in 1895, Ann Strong wrote, 'The bicycle is just as good company as most husbands and, when it gets old and shabby, a woman can dispose of it and get a new one without shocking the entire community.'

7. IT'S GREEN

↘ If we don't want our children to swim to work in the future, we're going to have to cut back on carbon-spewing forms of transport. Bicycles are one answer. Meandering down country lanes and exploring new territory by bike is so much more enjoyable than getting a 'cheap' flight to an airport hours away from where you actually want to go, at a far higher price than advertised.

8. IT CAN CARRY YOUR BAGS

↘ A bicycle can be quite the packhorse. With the right panniers, you can transport far more shopping than you would ever manage on foot. Add a trailer, and you could move house.

9. IT WILL SHOW YOU NEW THINGS

↘ Travelling by bike rather than by car, you experience the world differently. The view from the saddle is much better than from behind the wheel. Not only can you travel along towpaths and through forests closed to cars, but you can smell the flowers and hear the animals and birds as you go.

10. IT CAN TAKE YOU ANYWHERE YOU LIKE

↘ Riding a bike doesn't just free you from the tyranny of public transport, it also offers almost endless travel opportunities. Whether you want to cycle to a country pub, over to a friend's house or across continents, the only thing that will hold you back is your legs.

FROM THE VELOCIPEDE TO THE VELODROME: A POTTED HISTORY OF BICYCLES AND BICYCLING

1817 Baron Karl Friedrich invents the *draisienne* or hobby horse, the first practical attempt to use two wheels for personal transport. The machine has no pedals, but is propelled by the rider sitting astride the central seat and taking exaggerated steps along the road.

1839 Scottish blacksmith Kirkpatrick Macmillan invents a bicycle-like machine that is operated by the rider pushing up and down on pedal-like 'treadles', which he uses to cycle the 71 miles from his home in Dumfries to Glasgow. He fails to patent his invention and many others develop his design and take the credit. (NB: some people insist none of this ever happened and that the whole Macmillan story is a hoax.)

1861 Frenchman Pierre Michaux develops a more sophisticated pedal-driven bicycle, the velocipede. Velocipedomania begins. Indoor riding academies, similar to rollerskating rinks, become all the rage in large cities.

1868 An article in *Once a Week* on 21 March 1868 describes Paris as being 'inflicted with a serious nuisance: velocipedes, machines like the ghosts of departed spiders on which horrible boys and detestable men career about the streets and boulevards'.

1869 'Velocipedists are imbeciles on wheels!' declares French newspaper *Le Gaulois*.

1870s The ordinary, aka the penny-farthing, comes into circulation.

1884 The modern bicycle as we know it starts to appear on the streets with the invention of the Rover 'safety' bicycle.

1888 John Boyd Dunlop invents an air-filled inflatable tyre.

1894 The first bicycle couriers open for business in California when a railway strike halts mail delivery for the San Francisco Bay area.

1896 American civil rights activist Susan B. Anthony says, 'Let me tell you what I think of bicycling. I think it has done more to emancipate women than anything else in the world. I stand and rejoice every time I see a woman ride by on a wheel. It gives women a feeling of freedom and self-reliance.' Tessie Reynolds, a feisty sixteen-year-old, scandalizes the UK by riding a men's bicycle from Brighton to London and back wearing 'rational' dress.

1898 Lady Harberton, the founder and president of the Rational Dress Society, tries unsuccessfully to sue the landlady of a pub in Surrey who refuses to serve her while she is wearing her rational bicycling gear.

1903 First ever Tour de France held.

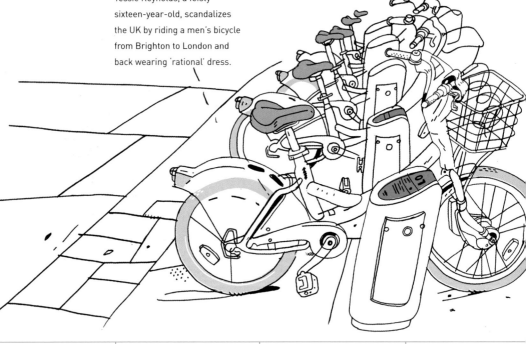

1981 Specialized's Stumpjumper becomes the first mass-produced mountain bike.

1993 'The Flying Scotsman' Graeme Obree sets world record by cycling further than anyone else in an hour on a bike he built from, among other things, a washing-machine part.

1995 Work starts on Britain's National Cycle Network.

1999 Lance Armstrong wins the Tour de France less than eighteen months after his last chemotherapy treatment for testicular cancer.

930s Bicycling experiences boom during the Depression; 1936, there are an estimated 1 million regular cyclists Britain.

1968 Raleigh invents the Chopper.

1973/4 Cycling is a beneficiary of the energy crisis, when several European countries ban Sunday pleasure-motoring, leaving the roads free for bicycling.

1980s Cycling shorts become fashionable off the bike.

005 Lance Armstrong retires fter winning his seventh onsecutive Tour de France.

2007 Paris launches a city-wide bike-rental scheme, the Vélib'.

2008 British cyclists dominate the Olympic velodrome in Beijing, winning fourteen medals, including eight golds.

2009 Manx racing cyclist Mark Cavendish becomes Britain's greatest Tour de France rider, winning six stages.

HOW TO BUY A BIKE

There are few feelings more glorious than finding the perfect bike and riding off on it into the sunset. When you've found the one, you'll know. Not only will you never want to go back to what you had before, but you'll have a hard time working out what you ever saw in it in the first place.

But as is so often the case when chasing an ideal, the quest can sometimes be arduous, especially if it's unfocused. To find the right bike, you need to know what you want. Before you start mooning over dreamy bicycles you see in shop windows and whizzing past you in the street, ask yourself the following five questions:

1. WHAT DO YOU PRIMARILY WANT TO USE THE BIKE FOR?

↘ Do you just want to ride your bike to work? Or are you planning a long trek, or maybe a charity bike ride? Will any of your routes be off-road, even if they are only gravelly towpaths? This all makes a difference to the sort of tyres you need, how many gears will be necessary and how much you should spend.

2. WHERE ARE YOU GOING TO STORE IT?

↘ Do you have a secure shed? A downstairs hallway where you can prop your bike? Or will you have to lug your new friend up several flights of stairs? If your bike is too heavy to carry to safety, you will use it less often. And if it is very expensive, you'll not want to leave it chained up outside.

3. DO YOU WANT TO WEAR YOUR ORDINARY CLOTHES WHILE RIDING IT?

↘ You can wear whatever you like on any bike, but cycling in civvies can be a much easier, more pleasant experience on certain types of bike. If you are a woman who likes to cycle in skirts and dresses, you might find life easier with a 'step-through' frame. If you don't fancy getting oily calves or trousers, a chain guard is a good idea.

4. DO YOU NEED TO BE ABLE TO CARRY STUFF WHILE YOU CYCLE?

↘ If you do, you will need a bike that can take a rear or front luggage rack, or handlebars that can hold a basket. Not all bikes can accommodate these things.

5. HOW MUCH DO YOU WANT TO SPEND?

↘ The big question. Spend what you can afford. If you want a second-hand bike, you can buy something decent for £100. There is a detailed guide to buying pre-loved bikes later in this chapter. If we're talking shiny and new, accept the fact that you're going to have to part with £300 or more. Once you have decided on your budget, stick to it. Don't let a charming sales assistant flatter you into buying something you'll be paying for until the end of time. Remember that you may qualify' for the government's 'Cycle to Work' scheme, which offers a hefty discount on a bicycle for your commute. See p. 196 for details.

When you have answered these five questions, you are in a much better position to buy the right bike for you. The following pages explore the main types of bicycle you are likely to encounter on your shopping expedition. Knowing which sort might suit you best will help you enormously when you walk into the shop or start browsing online.

Later in the chapter, I'll explain some of the technical stuff about brakes, gears and frame materials which you might well come across as you shop, and I'll also try and answer some common quandaries, such as 'Do you get what you pay for?', 'Can I cope with a crossbar?', 'How do I buy secondhand?' and 'Is it OK to buy a bike from a big chain store?'

THE DUTCH BIKE

[AKA THE VINTAGE BIKE, UPRIGHT BIKE, SIT-UP-AND-BEG BIKE, UTILITY BIKE OR THE ROADSTER]

If you are looking for a stylish, traditional bike to ride to work or to the shops, the Dutch bike might just be for you. Until recently, it was difficult to get hold of one of these retro beauties, but now even the big chains are selling them. Expect to pay £250–£750 for a new model. The big downer with these bikes is their weight. Many weigh 20kg (44lb) or more, which is fine for barrelling along a flat road but hard work up hills and a real pain if you don't live on the ground floor. More modern-looking models – such as those made by Germany's Fahrrad Manufaktur – are a lot lighter, so shop around if weight is an issue.

PROS

- Comfortable to ride over short distances
- Upright position gives a great view of the road
- Beautiful to look at
- Good for carrying stuff
- Perfect for short commutes, as they are often fitted with a chain guard, dress guard and mudguards to keep your clothes clean
- No crossbar on the women's version, so you can mount the saddle in a skirt without showing the world your knickers
- Most use hub gears, which are hidden inside the wheel hub, making them less sensitive to the elements. Hub gears can be changed when you are freewheeling or stationary, which is often easier for less experienced riders
- Very sturdy machines, which can cope with gravel, grass and potholes

CONS

- Often reeeeally heavy, so bad news if you have to carry it up stairs and almost impossible to hang up on a wall as storage
- Slow and hard work going up hills
- With many brands, you're paying more for the look than for the components
- Hub gears are very difficult to fix yourself
- Many don't have quick-release wheels, so it can be a trial fixing punctures
- Very big frames and wide handlebars take up a lot of space, so bad if your only safe storage option is a narrow corridor

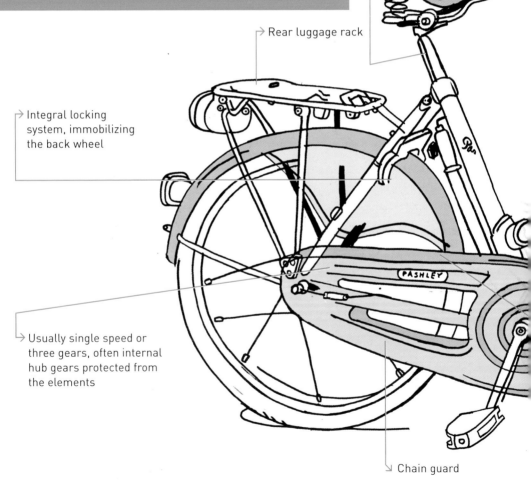

→ Upright riding position

→ Wide, comfy saddle

→ Rear luggage rack

→ Integral locking system, immobilizing the back wheel

→ Usually single speed or three gears, often internal hub gears protected from the elements

↘ Chain guard

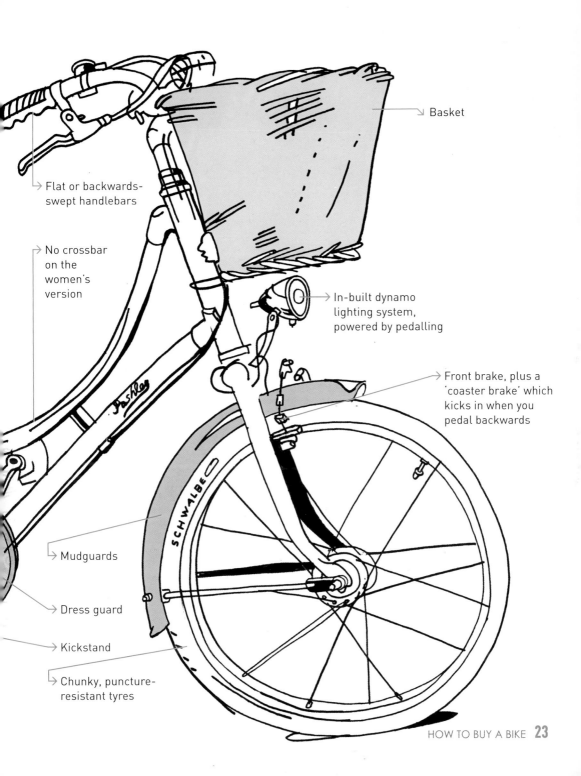

Basket

Flat or backwards-swept handlebars

No crossbar on the women's version

In-built dynamo lighting system, powered by pedalling

Front brake, plus a 'coaster brake' which kicks in when you pedal backwards

Mudguards

Dress guard

Kickstand

Chunky, puncture-resistant tyres

SCHWALBE

THE HYBRID BIKE

[AKA THE CITY BIKE, TOWN BIKE, CROSS BIKE, OR COMMUTER]

So called because it is a happy mix of mountain and road bike, the hybrid is great for commuters who might also want to do a bit of leisure or fitness riding at the weekends. Generally, it offers the comfort and ease of a vintage bike but without the weight – though it is a far less handsome machine. The *Guardian* columnist Zoe Williams once referred to it as 'the bike equivalent of elasticated trouser', which sums up the hybrid's lack of street cred rather brilliantly. Expect to pay £200–£700 for a new model.

PROS

- Quite cheap for what you get
- Easy to ride
- Durable
- Flexible – good for commuting as well as weekend adventuring
- Lighter and faster than the Dutch bike

CONS

- Often rather ugly and usually come in very boring colours
- Generally come with derailleur gears, which is a system of sprockets (bike-speak for cogs) and pulleys. Good for getting a good range of gears, but makes it difficult to fit a chain guard and more likely to be affected by adverse weather
- Their neither one thing nor t'other nature can be a disadvantage if you find you want to use the bike for sport

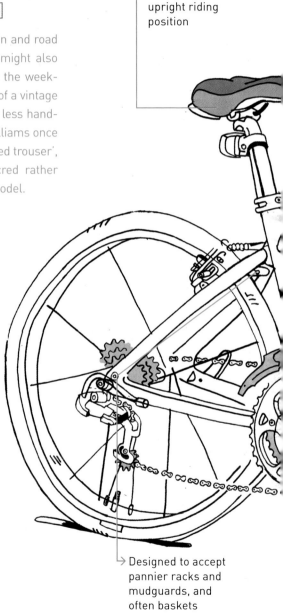

→ Relatively upright riding position

→ Designed to accept pannier racks and mudguards, and often baskets

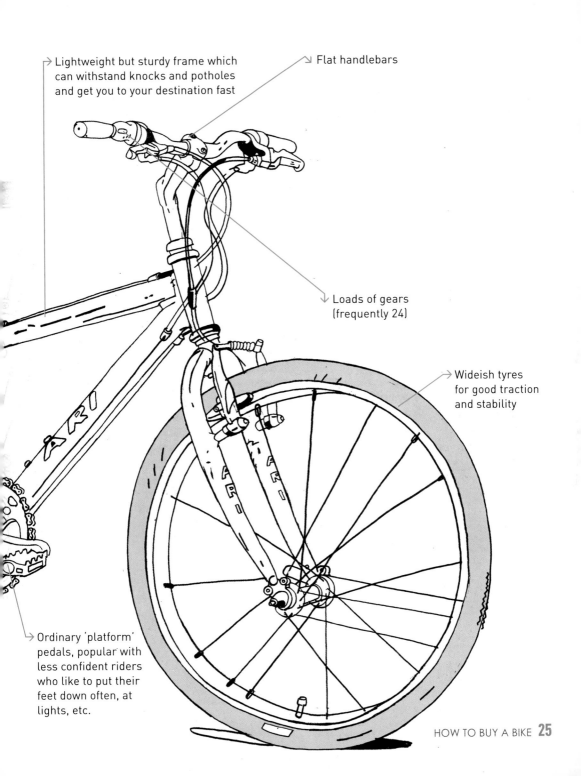

→ Lightweight but sturdy frame which
can withstand knocks and potholes
and get you to your destination fast

↘ Flat handlebars

↓ Loads of gears
(frequently 24)

→ Wideish tyres
for good traction
and stability

→ Ordinary 'platform'
pedals, popular with
less confident riders
who like to put their
feet down often, at
lights, etc.

THE FOLDING BIKE

The market for folding bikes has exploded in the past few years, and no wonder – these clever machines make commuting a doddle by cleverly foiling the infuriating 'no bikes on public transport' rule. When a bicycle is folded, it becomes luggage, giving one in the eye to bike-hating transport planners. For the lowdown on taking bikes on trains and planes, see chapter 8.

A folder costs £200–£2,000 or even more (and occasionally less), but bear in mind that the cheapest models often fold awkwardly and ride badly. Expect to pay £400-plus for a decent specimen which folds nicely and isn't too heavy or cumbersome to carry around with you, and twice that if you want something that feels like a 'proper' bike to ride. If it is any consolation, folders depreciate far less than standard bicycles, so you can generally sell them on at not too great a loss when you've had enough. Because you never leave your bike alone, it is far less likely to get stolen too. Think twice before leaving a folder locked up anywhere. Their high resale value makes them very attractive to thieves.

If you want a bike which folds up small enough to take on trains and planes as hand luggage, you will probably have to live with small (16 or 18 inch) wheels. Some people find this a bit of a trial, as it means your legs will have to go round faster in order to sustain a sensible speed. Bikes with bigger wheels can give a smoother ride, but they tend to just fold in half and so are only useful for stuffing in car boots or hallways (though some are too big to fit in the boot of small cars). If you are going to be folding and unfolding your bike regularly, make sure it is one which is quick and easy to assemble – Brompton folders transform from luggage to bicycle in less than thirty seconds. Manufacturers often give wildly optimistic folding times in the product specifications, so try before you buy, if possible. Some, such as the electric GoCycle, or Moultons, don't actually fold at all but can be taken to bits fairly easily.

It's a good idea to try a number of different models before taking the plunge: there really are radical differentiations between folders and, although they are, theoretically, one size fits all, the reality is that they will suit some people far better than others. Some, particularly those which fold into the smallest package, feel very rickety to ride.

Folders are not necessarily only for short jaunts. While doing the Dunwich Dynamo, a 120-mile overnight ride from east London to the Sussex coast, I was passed by a number of Bromptons. I couldn't quite work out how that was possible, given my wheels were twice the size, but there you go. Bromptons, incidentally, almost always come top of the list when folders are put to the test. You can also buy folding tandems – German brand Bernds makes a well regarded model.

Most ordinary bike shops still don't stock folders and, if they do, there will usually be a very limited range. You are best off doing some sleuthing on the internet and finding the dealer nearest you, and making a day of it to test ride a few. There is a very good guide to buying a folding bike on the A to B magazine website (www.atob.org.uk), which includes a directory of UK shops specializing in folding bikes. The Folding Society is quite a handy (if nerdy) website for enthusiasts and novices alike, and includes detailed discussions of the joys and foibles of different models: www.foldsoc.co.uk

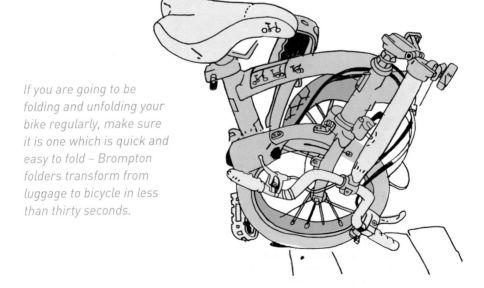

If you are going to be folding and unfolding your bike regularly, make sure it is one which is quick and easy to fold – Brompton folders transform from luggage to bicycle in less than thirty seconds.

PROS

↘ Perfect for commutes that involve a leg on public transport

↘ Great for people who live in flats, as they are easy to carry up stairs and don't take up much room

↘ Never need be locked up outside, so almost thief-proof

↘ Can be flung in a car without the need for a roof- or boot-rack

↘ Step-through frame makes wearing skirts practical, and means the bike is easy to mount for people with hip or back problems

CONS

↘ Cheap models are rubbish

↘ Decent models are still very expensive

↘ For the same price, you could buy a really classy ordinary bike which is far nicer to ride

↘ Small wheel folders in particular often feel unstable, so unsuitable for novice riders

↘ Lack of gear range can make longer rides on rolling terrain a bit of a night-mare

↘ Can be difficult to find panniers, baskets and other accessories to fit

↘ You need to carry tools to fold up some bikes, particularly the more expensive models with big wheels

BRANDS TO INVESTIGATE INCLUDE:

↘ **AirFrame** (British): www.airframebike.com

↘ **Airnimal** (British): www.airnimal.com

↘ **Bernds** (German): www.bernds.de

↘ **Bike Friday** (American): www.bikefriday.com

↘ **Birdy** (American): www.birdybike.com

↘ **Brompton** (British): www.brompton.co.uk

↘ **Dahon** (American): www.dahon.co.uk

↘ **GoCycle** (British): www.gocycle.com

↘ **Mezzo** (British): www.mezzobikes.com

↘ **Moulton** (British): www.moultonbicycles.co.uk

↘ **Strida** (Dutch): www.strida.co.uk

→ Some have wheels so that you can drag them along like a suitcase

→ Some folders are single speed; most have three to seven gears

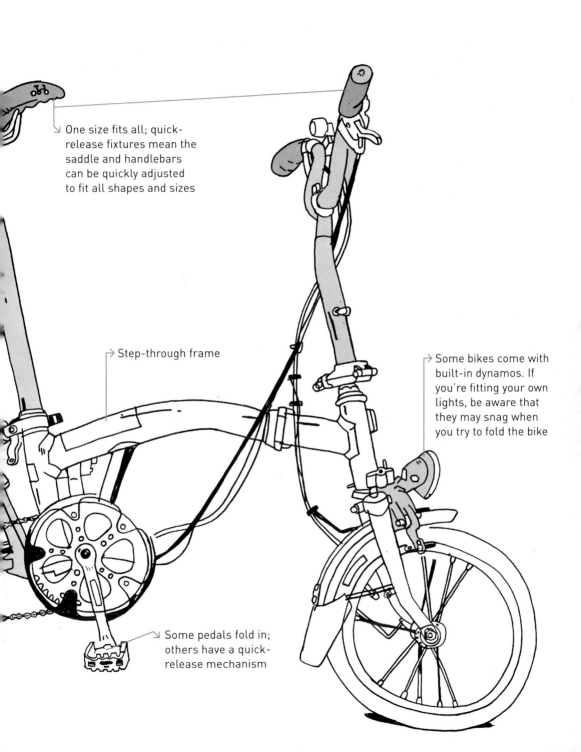

One size fits all; quick-release fixtures mean the saddle and handlebars can be quickly adjusted to fit all shapes and sizes

→ Step-through frame

→ Some bikes come with built-in dynamos. If you're fitting your own lights, be aware that they may snag when you try to fold the bike

Some pedals fold in; others have a quick-release mechanism

THE ROAD BIKE

[AKA A RACER]

If speed is your priority, and you've got a bit of cash to splash, a nippy racer might be the answer. They are really designed for longer, faster rides, with drop handlebars (the curly ones that look like ram's horns), lightweight frames and nimble, thin tyres, but you can easily commute on one. My main bike is a racer, and most of the time I have it fitted with a rack to carry luggage, and clip-on mudguards to keep my legs clean. Prices for entry-level road bikes start from £500, but you can spend an infinite amount, so beware of getting too carried away. If you're looking to cycle further than to work and back, you might want to consider having a bike custom made, but it won't come cheap. Around £200 will buy you a really decent secondhand racer.

→ Usually come with a small saddle

→ Wide range of gears, usually eighteen upwards

→ Skinny, slick tyres

↘ Large wheels, which are good for covering long distances

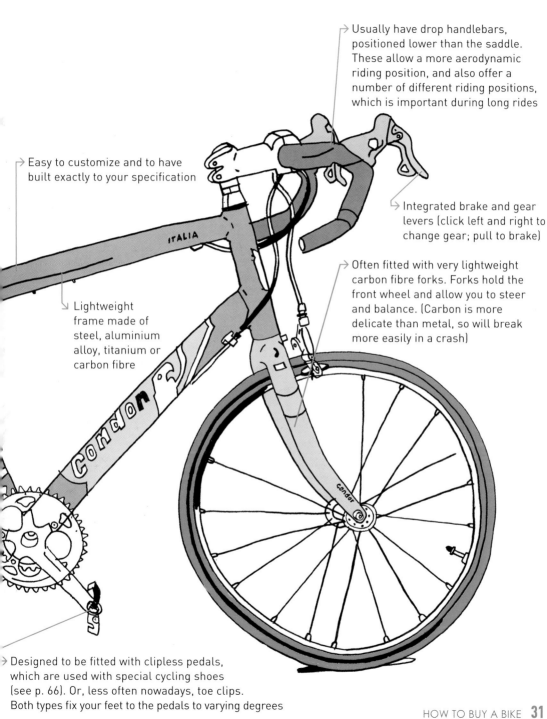

Usually have drop handlebars, positioned lower than the saddle. These allow a more aerodynamic riding position, and also offer a number of different riding positions, which is important during long rides

Easy to customize and to have built exactly to your specification

Integrated brake and gear levers (click left and right to change gear; pull to brake)

Often fitted with very lightweight carbon fibre forks. Forks hold the front wheel and allow you to steer and balance. (Carbon is more delicate than metal, so will break more easily in a crash)

Lightweight frame made of steel, aluminium alloy, titanium or carbon fibre

ITALIA

condor

condor

Designed to be fitted with clipless pedals, which are used with special cycling shoes (see p. 66). Or, less often nowadays, toe clips. Both types fix your feet to the pedals to varying degrees

CONS

↘ Thin, slick tyres are prone to punctures (though you can easily replace these with puncture-resistant models)

↘ Small saddle and drop handlebars often make for a less comfortable ride. Some people don't like stretching down to brake

↘ Not great in wet weather, because the mechanisms – the derailleur gears and brakes – are open to the elements

↘ Skinny tyres don't cope well off-road, or even on gravel. You'll feel every lump and bump

↘ Not always possible to attach a rack. If that matters to you, before you buy, check there are bosses (eyelets) built into the frame to allow you to do so

You can buy road bikes off the peg from most bike shops, or more specialist outlets will customize a model for you by taking your exact measurements and aesthetic requirements into consideration.

PROS

↘ Fast

↘ Lovely and light, so great if you have to carry up stairs

↘ Very efficient machines, so less hard work to pedal than other types

↘ Easy to upgrade and fiddle with; should last for ever if looked after

↘ You can use for sport (triathlons, sportives) as well as for leisure and commuting

THE MOUNTAIN BIKE

Designed for going off-road, mountain bikes nevertheless remain popular as commuter bikes. They have sturdy frames, flat, knobbly tyres, powerful brakes and are very easy to manoeuvre at low speeds. They are cumbersome beasts, however, and come fitted with all sorts of bits and bobs you'll never need on the road. The cheapest models on the market come in this category. You can spend as little as £70 on a new – but seriously suboptimal – machine in supermarkets, as you will shortly see; but for something half decent that could actually cope off-road, you're looking at spending at least £400. If, realistically, you aren't going to do any actual mountain biking, resist a machine with loads of suspension and other whistles and bells. If you want to go off-road, you will need a bike with 'full suspension' on both front and rear, or just a 'hardtail' (no rear suspension). Full suspension bikes are usually more comfortable and easier to control compared with hardtail machines, though they are heavier, require more maintenance and cost quite a bit more.

PROS

- ↘ Easy to ride
- ↘ Can be very cheap
- ↘ Good for rough terrain
- ↘ Cope well with potholes and the like
- ↘ Can be used for commuting as well as off-roading on the weekend

CONS

- ↘ Cheap models are rubbish
- ↘ Often very heavy
- ↘ Thick tyres make for a slow ride
- ↘ Not always possible to attach pannier rack, basket, etc.

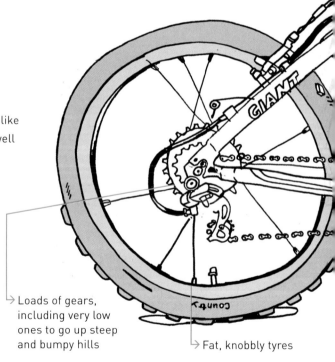

→ Loads of gears, including very low ones to go up steep and bumpy hills

→ Fat, knobbly tyres

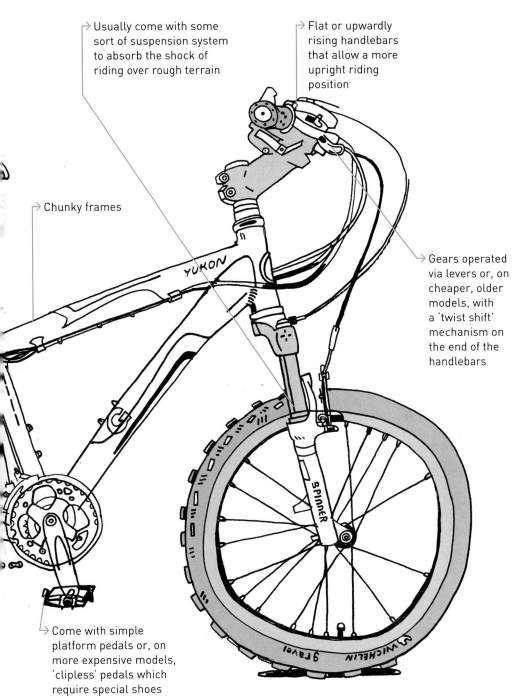

Usually come with some sort of suspension system to absorb the shock of riding over rough terrain

Flat or upwardly rising handlebars that allow a more upright riding position

Chunky frames

YUKON

Gears operated via levers or, on cheaper, older models, with a 'twist shift' mechanism on the end of the handlebars

SPINNER

WICHELIN gravel

Come with simple platform pedals or, on more expensive models, 'clipless' pedals which require special shoes

THE FIXED GEAR BIKE

[AKA A FIXIE, A FIXED WHEEL BIKE]

These sleek, minimalist machines are based on track bikes used by competitive cyclists at velodromes, and have long been popular with cycle couriers, who need reliable machines with as few things to go wrong as possible. Increasingly, though, they are being ridden by ordinary, style-conscious folk who use their 'fixies' as more of a fashion accessory than a mode of transport. A whole sub-culture has grown up around fixed gear bikes, with magazines, books and websites devoted to fixie worshipping.

Just one front chain ring and one sprocket (cog) on the rear, which does not freewheel. When you pedal, the bike moves; when you don't, it doesn't

Jazzy colour schemes

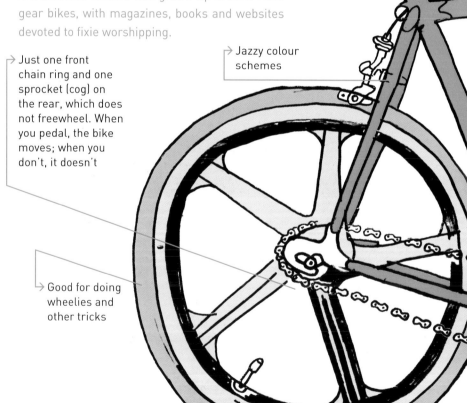

Good for doing wheelies and other tricks

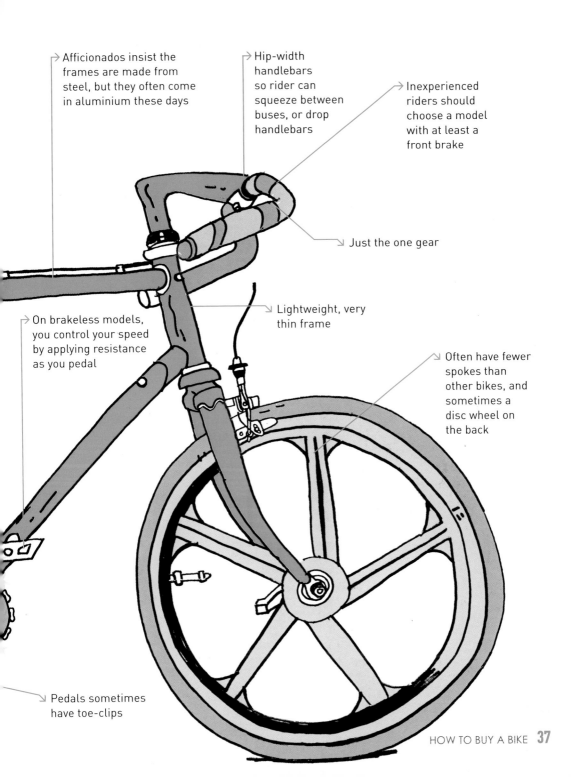

Afficionados insist the frames are made from steel, but they often come in aluminium these days

Hip-width handlebars so rider can squeeze between buses, or drop handlebars

Inexperienced riders should choose a model with at least a front brake

Just the one gear

On brakeless models, you control your speed by applying resistance as you pedal

Lightweight, very thin frame

Often have fewer spokes than other bikes, and sometimes a disc wheel on the back

Pedals sometimes have toe-clips

A true fixed gear bike is single-speed with no freewheel and no brakes, but most used on the roads these days have a brake at the front but not at the back. Not having a freewheel means you can't coast – the wheels only turn when you pedal. You never get a rest, even if going downhill, and if the incline is too steep on the way up, you can't change down a gear. The advantage of this is that your muscles don't seize up or get tight and you get a great workout. Many models also have narrow handlebars, which make it easier to squeeze through queues of traffic – a big plus or a dangerous incitement, depending on your point of view.

Until recently, most fixed gear bikes seen out on the open road were conversions from track or road bikes, but now you can buy ready-made models from companies such as Charge. This is a better idea, because their geometry is suited to the road – because they never have to take sharp corners, track bikes tend to be very compact and therefore people can find the front wheel hits their toes when cornering in the real world.

Expect to pay upwards of £400 for a half decent bike. You can buy off the peg or get one customized with wheels, tyres, chains, frames and handlebar tape in all the colours of the rainbow from dedicated bike builders. Create Bikes in London creates new fixed gear bikes from old bike parts and will customize them in the colour scheme of your choice (www.createbikes.com). It is also possible to convert some ordinary road bikes into a fixie, should you so wish.

Fixed gear bikes are not recommended for novice cyclists, and if you take the plunge, expect to take a while to get used to not being able to freewheel. Once you do, though, devotees insist you feel a closer communion with your bike and with the road, and will develop a better riding style. They like to bang on about the 'purity' of the experience too, and of being 'at one' with their bicycle. It definitely makes you fit – I know fixie riders who can go 100 miles or more across hilly terrain. Being strapped into the pedals also makes for a more efficient ride. Very little power is lost and much is gained in the upstroke.

Though it defeats the object rather, some new fixed gear bikes can be converted to a freewheeling single speed by putting the back wheel on the other way around with what is quaintly called a 'flip-flop hub'.

There are no shortage of websites and forums discussing all things fixie. A good place to start is London Fixed Gear and Single Speed (www.londonfgss.com). Despite its focus on the capital, the forum holds the answer to just about every fixed gear question you could imagine.

PROS

↘ Very lightweight, so good for anyone who lives up several flights of stairs

↘ With no gears to maintain, there are fewer bits to look after

↘ The fixed gear is good at very low speeds, so you can stay upright while waiting for a chance to jump through traffic or simply balance at the lights without putting your foot down

↘ Very customizable; can be ordered in every colour of the rainbow

↘ Good exercise, as you never stop pedalling and have to work hard on hills – both up and down

↘ Because you are more solidly connected to the bike, you have better control of it in bumpy conditions or on difficult corners

↘ They look cool – the very essence of a bicycle, with no superfluous bits

CONS

↘ Not great for going up hills – though fixed gear fans swear their bikes are surprisingly good climbers

↘ No rear brake means lots of skid stops, which wears down the rear tyre more quickly

↘ Style over substance; often really expensive for what they are

↘ Tend to have no eyelets to attach any extras, whether a pannier rack, bottle cage or basket

↘ Skinny tyres mean you'll really feel the potholes

↘ No freewheel for when you're going downhill or get tired and want to coast

Purists like to flaunt their anti-establishment credentials on home-built bikes with no branding. Sensing money to be made, however, the biggest bike manufacturers, such as Trek and Giant, have all brought out fixed gear models, and you can increasingly buy fixies from the major bike chains.

SOME SPECIALIST OUTLETS, MANUFACTURERS AND BIKE BUILDERS INCLUDE:

↘ **14 Bike Co., London:** http://14bikeco.wordpress.com

↘ **Brick Lane Bikes, London:** http://bricklanebikes.co.uk

↘ **Charge Bikes:** www.chargebikes.com

↘ **Create:** www.createbikes.com

↘ **Fixie Inc:** www.cycles-for-heroes.com

↘ **Tokyo Fixed Gear:** www.tokyofixedgear.com

If you know you want a particular sort of bike, e.g. a Dutch bike or a fixed gear model, seek out a shop specializing in these sorts of machines.

OTHER KINDS OF BIKES

SHOPPERS (AKA GRANNY BIKES)

These dainty numbers have a step-through frame and tiny wheels, and are usually accessorized with a basket on the front and a little bike box on the back. You almost never see them new any more, but they can be picked up very cheaply secondhand or, just as often, out of a skip. They are fine for pootling around town and are unlikely to get stolen, as they are wholly unattractive to bike thieves. But if you want to upgrade or replace bits, you'll have a job finding components to fit.

STREET BIKES

Essentially racing bikes with flat handlebars, allowing a more upright riding position, which is helpful in traffic. They also often have stronger wheels than your classic racer, and are designed to be able to fit mudguards and luggage racks.

TOURING BIKES

Built for comfort and strength, tourers are designed to carry a lot of luggage over long distances. They look like racers, but generally come with pannier rack and mudguards as standard and have sturdier tyres and wheels, should you go off-road, as well as a much comfier saddle. Audax bikes are very similar to tourers. They are used for Audax events – long distance rides in which competitors have to cycle to checkpoints by certain times.

RECUMBENT BIKES

Popular among people with bad backs, recumbent riders sit near the ground in a go-karting sort of position, pounding the pedals with their legs almost horizontal. These machines are surprisingly speedy, because they encounter less air resistance, though they are not ideal for riding in traffic and are not great for going uphill, as you can't press your body weight on the pedals.

BMX

Very popular in the eighties, a little more niche these days, BMX bikes are designed for performing tricks and riding on special circuits rather than for everyday cycling.

CYCLOCROSS

Ridden by mad people who like competing in events which combine cross-country running and cycling, these bikes look a bit like racers but have knobbly tyres for going off-road. They are very light, as they are designed to be slung over the shoulder.

TRIATHLON

Lightweight, aerodynamic road bikes with special 'tri-bar' handlebars fitted at the front on which the rider can lean their elbows when going fast. These are often fitted with a disc wheel, which has solid sides instead of spokes. Note that you can fit tri-bars to most normal racers if you do a triathlon and don't want to buy a whole new bike especially.

ELECTRIC BIKES

Electric bikes are becoming ever more popular, and the designs have improved massively of late. They're very handy if you live somewhere hilly or if your knees aren't quite what they used to be. Or, of course, if you're just a lazy so-and-so. E-bikes can be ridden as an ordinary bike and usually have a switch or button on the handlebars that starts the electric-assist when your legs get tired or you can't be bothered pedalling. They are often very heavy, so not great if you have to carry them up stairs; and check carefully how long the battery lasts and how easy it is to recharge. The other downer – for the more superficial aesthetes, at least – is that most of them look really ugly. This is changing, with space-agey models such as the GoCycle, however. Note: in the UK, legally, you have to be fourteen to ride an electric bike. Again, A to B magazine is a great source of information on e-bikes (www.atob.org.uk).

HANDCYCLES

Handcycles are ridden by wheelchair users or other people with limited use of their legs. They can be easily mounted and are powered by the upper body.

TANDEMS

A bicycle made for two. They are expensive, and a nightmare to store, but enormous fun to use. Generally, the stronger rider goes at the front (in tandem speak, this is being the Captain) and does all the steering. If you don't want to buy a new tandem, scour the classifieds in cycling magazines for secondhand models.

BIKE-BUYING FAQS

Q· DO YOU GET WHAT YOU PAY FOR?

↘ Up to a point, yes. More expensive bikes have better quality components and lighter frames and forks made out of carbon fibre or titanium, which will make them quicker and slicker to ride. But if you're not bothered about going particularly fast and never anticipate having to lug your bike up stairs or over railway bridges, you'll be wasting your money on a top-notch machine. Light doesn't always equal best – if your route to work is strewn with potholes, you'll want something sturdy to cope with it, and the heavier it is, the less nickable it is too.

Sometimes, you pay extra simply because the bike looks cool. The style over substance problem tends to plague the fixed-gear and Dutch bike market most. That said, there is no point buying a really cheap new bike. Buy cheap, buy twice – as I discovered road testing 'Britain's cheapest bike'.

Test riding Britain's cheapest bike

In 2009, the supermarket Asda began selling what it called 'Britain's cheapest bike'. For just £70, customers could walk away with a brand-new adult's bike. I decided to get hold of one – an eighteen-speed British Eagle mountain bike in a girlish purple shade.

My first outing on the Purple Eagle ended on a sour note when the handlebars started turning in an entirely unhelpful way every time I rounded a corner. The headset – the bit which attaches the handlebars to the frame – was horribly loose, and I had no tools on me to fix it. Herein lies the first problem with buying what bike snobs refer to as a BSO (bike-shaped object): you have to build it yourself. The Eagle comes in bits, meaning you have to attach the pedals, front wheel, handlebars and saddle to the frame. Are you sure you know how to put it together? If not, you can either take it to your local bike dealer and hope they won't laugh you out of the shop when you ask them to do it for you (and if they oblige, you'll pay at least £20 for it), or risk getting it wrong.

The second problem was the flimsy grip-shift gears, which are operated by twisting the end of the handlebars. Every time I went over a speed bump I changed gear; even on the flat, there was always an irritating clicking sound which spoiled every ride. The problems didn't end there. The pedals and brakes were plastic, rather than metal, and so sure to wear out within weeks. And despite being a ladies' bike, it came with a torturously uncomfortable men's saddle. The front wheel wasn't even properly round. When I wheeled it into my local bike shop, the owner groaned – 'We see these a couple of times a week, and so often the repairs cost more than the bike,' he said, adding that he gave me 'four to six weeks' before the bike was too jiggered to ride.

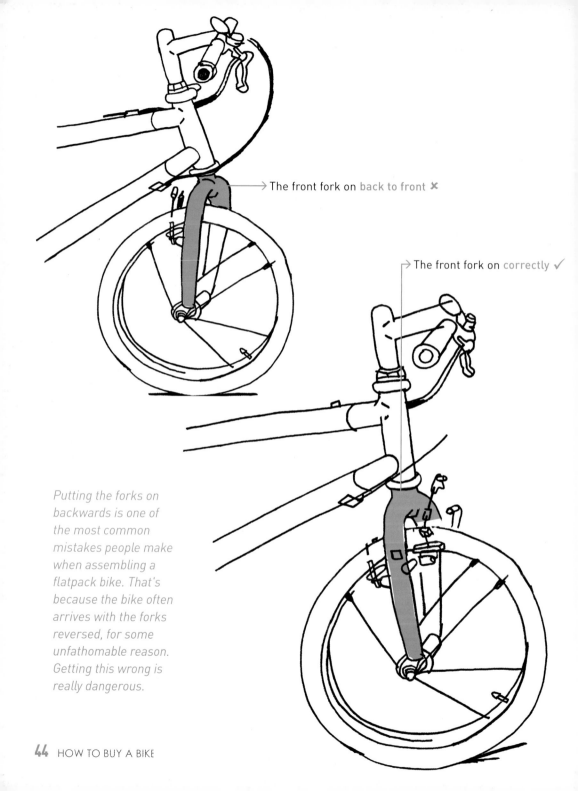

→ The front fork on back to front ✗

→ The front fork on correctly ✓

Putting the forks on backwards is one of the most common mistakes people make when assembling a flatpack bike. That's because the bike often arrives with the forks reversed, for some unfathomable reason. Getting this wrong is really dangerous.

Q· DO I NEED GEARS?

↘ When I was growing up, my friends and I all believed the more gears our bikes boasted the better – 'Yours has only got eighteen? Mine has twenty-four' went our conversations, until somebody claimed to have a billion trillion gears. But most people don't need all that many. For general pootling about, three are often enough; perhaps seven at a push. I have twenty-four on my road bike and regularly use only about eight of them. Although single speed bikes have experienced a bit of a renaissance of late, gears remain a handy thing for a bike to have. If you live near a big hill, it's good to have a low gear to get to the summit and a high one to race down it and along the flats.

There are two common gear systems:

Hub gears

Most often used on Dutch bikes and folding bikes or other machines with no more than eight gears, hub gears are encased within the hub of the bicycle's rear wheel. Gears are changed by a cable, which is tightened or loosened by a lever or twist grip on the handlebars. They need less maintenance than derailleurs because the mechanism is sealed in the hub, and you can change gear even if you're not pedalling – this is useful if you find yourself sitting at traffic lights in too high a gear to pedal off. The other advantage is that hub gears can be covered with a chain guard, protecting your clothes from oil and grease, and the chain won't come off. But if something goes wrong, they're a nightmare to mend, and you usually get a low gear ratio, which means you don't have a wide range of gears to play with when switching between hills and fast, flat stretches. NB: sometimes hub gears are called Sturmey Archers, the brand name of one of the first widely manufactured types. A particularly flashy kind of hub gear is made by the German manufacturer Rohloff, which offers fourteen gears.

Derailleur gears

Commonly used on bikes with more than three gears, the derailleur system consists of a rear derailleur and front derailleur controlled by levers or twist grips on the handlebars. The rear mech (short for 'mechanism', but always referred to as a 'mech') shifts the chain between sprockets/cogs on the back wheel; the front mech shifts between two or three chain rings attached to the crank arm, which is what your pedals are stuck on to. The big plus with derailleurs is that you get a wide range of gears, which means you are equally well disposed to climbing hills as bombing it along the flats. They are also relatively easy to tinker with.

Q. WHAT SORT OF BRAKES DO I NEED?

⬎ Any will do. Unless you're going to get a bike built to your specification, you'll likely have to live with whatever sort of brakes your bike comes with, which are probably one of these three types:

Calliper brakes

Common on road bikes, hybrids, Dutch bikes and folders, calliper brakes work by squeezing a lever on the handlebars. This forces the arms of the callipers to move together and make the brake pads squeeze the rim of the tyre. They are light and easy to maintain, but aren't so good in the rain.

Disc brakes

Originally used on motorbikes, disc brakes are used most often on mountain bikes ridden off-road, though you occasionally see them on other bicycles. Disc brakes consist of a metal disc attached to the wheel hub that rotates with the wheel. They work well in wet or muddy conditions and usually require less maintenance than rim brakes. The downer with these is that their design and positioning sometimes preclude the use of many types of luggage racks. They are also quite expensive.

Coaster brakes

Common on Dutch bikes, these are operated by pedalling backwards. Because the mechanism is not open to the elements, they perform well in rain or snow – but if something does go wrong, they're a pain to fix. They take some getting used to as well.

Q. WHAT'S THE POINT OF A CROSSBAR?

⊿ A crossbar, the tube which runs horizontally between the seat post and the handlebar stem on most bikes, is primarily there for engineering purposes: it makes the frame structurally more sound. Traditional ladies' bikes tend not to have a crossbar, but instead have a 'step-through' frame, designed back in the day so that the whole world didn't catch a glimpse of a woman's bloomers when she climbed aboard. It also facilitates that jaunty move you see postmen doing in films, where they ride with both feet on one side of the bike so they can hop on and off quickly.

There is no law decreeing that women should not ride bikes with crossbars, or that men may not benefit from a step-through frame. Anyone with back or hip problems will find it much easier to get on a bike without a crossbar. Unisex Dutch bikes tend not to have crossbars, and neither do folding bikes.

Q. SHOULD WOMEN BUY WOMEN'S BIKES?

⊿ Not necessarily. Everyone should buy a bike that fits them and suits their purposes. Ladies' bikes tend to have slightly different proportioned frames to take into account the fact women often have relatively longer torsos and shorter legs than men. They may also have a downward sloping crossbar, or no crossbar at all, and a special, wider saddle made to accommodate a womanly rear.

Q. DO I NEED SUSPENSION?

⊿ Only if you're planning on doing some serious off-roading. Suspension is used primarily on mountain bikes, but you occasionally see it implemented on road or hybrid bikes. It is unnecessary for urban riding, however many potholes or speed bumps you encounter on your commute.

BUYING A BIKE

THE BIKE SHOP

Now that you have an idea of what sort of bike you might like, you're ready to go shopping. Really, you should be punching the air at this prospect – after all, you're about to buy a beautiful new bicycle! But I bet a lot of you are thinking: gulp, now I have to go to a bike shop. To an outsider, these establishments can be terrifying places, stuffed full of a bewildering number of similar-looking machines with wildly varying price tags and unclear benefits. Not just that, but many are staffed by truculent young men with oily hands who either patronize you into submission or blind you with unnecessary cycling science. Recently, my friend Nic left her local branch of a national chain in fury after she went in to buy a new inner tube and was given an unsolicited lecture on how tyres work, all delivered using the analogy of a stiletto heel.

I think the journalist and bike nut Matt Seaton provides the best explanation for why some bike shop employees enjoy treating their customers like imbeciles:

Bikeshop boys take jobs in bikeshops because they love bikes and they get a good discount. But what they love most is playing with bikes and riding them, not selling them and, worse, answering questions about whether they've got a new nut to go on this bit, and do they know why the gears are making this noise, and, by the way, do they have a set of Allen keys to lend? For most of these young men, the compensation for the boredom of the retail routine and the frustration of dealing with all those idiotic customers is the opportunity to humiliate them in a multitude of ways.

From *The Escape Artist*, Matt Seaton

Of course, not all bike shops are like this. An increasing number have woken up to the fact that treating their customers with respect rather than contempt is actually rather a good business move. But there are all too many who will bark at you about gear ratios and group sets and insist you need to spend a grand on a bike that weighs less than a newborn when all you really want is a reliable machine to get you to the shops and back. If you encounter this sort of nonsense, up your heels and go elsewhere.

If you know you want a particular sort of bike – Dutch bikes or fixed gear spring to mind – try to seek out a shop specializing in those sorts of machines. Ordinary bike shops tend to just stock one or two niche models, and their employees may have no experience of riding them. You want to be served by people who can answer all your questions about the sort of bike you're interested in.

Assuming you have a choice of shops, only give your business to the ones who treat you like a sentient adult. Don't necessarily be put off by the fact that your chosen establishment doesn't have the bike of your dreams on sale. Your new friends may be able to order it in. Give them a précis of your answers to the five questions at the beginning of the chapter, and see what they have on offer.

Of course this works both ways – always be polite to people who work in bike shops. Generally, they are on more or less minimum wage, and though they would rather be out riding, they really would like to help you. I was flabbergasted to see how one man treated a female assistant at my local bike shop recently. He told her he wanted to see a mechanic. She told him she was a mechanic and asked how she could help. He said, no, a *real* mechanic.

THE TEST RIDE

The only way of really finding out whether a bike is for you is to give it a spin. Indeed, the best bike shops not only recommend you try out a bike before buying it, they insist on it. Expect to try out at least three before you find your perfect match. Usually, you'll have to give your credit card as surety in case you never return.

THE PERILS OF BUYING ONLINE

Sometimes people decide to skip the bike shop altogether and jump online instead. Be wary of doing this. First of all, you have no way of knowing whether the bike will really fit you. Even if you know your inside leg measurement to the nearest millimetre, there is no absolute standard between manufacturers – just like a size 10 in Marks & Spencer is bigger than a size 10 in Topshop. Not only will you not be able to try it out first, but if something goes wrong, you'll probably have to pay to get it fixed. If you buy from a proper shop, they'll more than likely offer a free service a month or so after you buy the bike, just to check everything is working properly. They'll also be far more inclined to fix it further on down the line – indeed, some over-subscribed shops will only fix bikes they themselves have sold.

Bikes bought over the internet also tend to arrive flatpacked, which we know from the Asda experiment is a recipe for disaster unless you really know what you're doing.

Of course, you could go to a real life shop, try out a bike and then buy it online if you think you can get it cheaper. But a better, more ethical, move would be to simply tell it like it is: explain to the sales assistant that you want the bike but can buy it cheaper online (a printout is a good idea). Very often they will match the price.

IS IT OK TO HAGGLE?

It's worth a go, especially if you have built up a rapport with the shop assistant. It's unusual to get a discount on the bike itself (apart from the automatic price reductions you often get if you are a member of a cycling organization such as the CTC), but very often you can wangle a cheaper helmet or lock, or maybe a free set of lights. You are more likely to succeed on this front if you are not in a chain store, though if you are polite and friendly and stick with the same assistant throughout the whole buying process, you might get lucky. At the end of the year, the previous season's bikes are often discounted. In bike years, this means that autumn/winter is often a good time to buy.

CHAIN STORE OR INDEPENDENT SHOP?

Do support independent bike shops, especially if they are local to you. Independent shops often offer superior service, because they tend to be managed by their owners, who really know their stuff and care whether you come again. At big chain stores, especially on the weekend, you sometimes get part-time workers who would just as happily work in Superdrug. They don't really care if you get the bike of your dreams, or if they sell you something totally unsuitable. They'll get the commission and, anyway, by the time you return to complain, they'll be back at college.

The downer is that small shops have a correspondingly small range of bikes. If you want to support your nearest shop but they don't have the machine you want, it's worth telling them your dilemma. Maybe they can order it in for you (though this isn't always possible, as many manufacturers insist on bulk ordering), or they can suggest something similar, or perhaps a model better than the one you were hankering after. If you can't buy your bike locally, make sure you pop in for all your other bikey needs. If you don't, they'll go out of business, and next time you just want to buy a new inner tube or a replacement for that screw you lost, you'll have to go all the way into town to Halfords.

Never buy a bike from a shop which doesn't specialize in bikes.

BUYING SECONDHAND

If you are short of cash but still want a good bike, buy secondhand. You'll probably get a far better used bike for £100 than you would spending £200 on something new and sub-standard. There are two main pitfalls with buying a used bike – 1. it's not always easy to tell whether the bike is any good, and 2. it can be hard to ascertain whether it has come from a reputable source.

How to spot a stolen bike

- ⬊ Never buy from a market stall. These are the prime locations for criminals offloading fenced goods, including bicycles.
- ⬊ If you are buying the bike from an individual, whether via eBay or a classified ad in a local paper, ask the owner to provide some proof of purchase. If they won't or say they can't, be suspicious. If they don't have a receipt, maybe they have insurance documents or the manual they got with the bike when it was new.
- ⬊ If you meet the owner, ask yourself whether the owner and the bike are a likely match. Could that kid really have been able to afford that top-end racing bike?
- ⬊ If not all the bike parts match, ask the owner why that's the case. Often, thieves strip down stolen bikes and mix and match the parts to make the provenance harder to trace; sometimes they've only nicked the frame and left the wheels. There are often legitimate reasons for mismatched componentry, but casually asking why this is the case could root out a dodgy dealer.
- ⬊ Check if the bike has any security markings. Look under the frame, underneath the bottom tube, and see if the serial number is intact. If someone has filed it off, walk away. Some bikes are postcoded. If the postcode doesn't match the seller, ask them why.
- ⬊ When you decide to buy, ask for a receipt. If they won't give you one, ask why.

Where to buy a secondhand bike

The most reputable places to buy secondhand are from a proper shop or a police auction, where the police sell off stolen bikes they cannot reunite with their true owners. To find your nearest auction, ask at your local police station or have a look on *www.bumblebeeauctions.co.uk*, where many forces sell their stuff. Others sub-contract out the sale to an auction house; you can find a list on www.police-information.co.uk.

Bike hire shops often sell their bikes on after a certain time at low cost too.

The biggest bargains are found at auctions, but the disadvantage is that you have to buy without inspecting the bike closely and have no comeback if you are sold a pup. Wherever you go, try to take along a bike-knowledgeable friend who can steer you away from disaster. Make sure you understand exactly how the bidding process works before you get cracking, and check that you don't have to register as a bidder beforehand. Remember that you will have to pay an auctioneer's fee in addition to the price of the bike – usually 10 per cent of the cost.

What to look for in a secondhand bike

There really is no point spending £25 on a bike only to discover that it's going to cost £150 to make it roadworthy. So learn to look for the obvious warning signs and get a test ride if possible, as secondhand bikes are usually sold 'as seen' (no refunds). Bear in mind that it can be very difficult to get hold of certain parts of old models, so if a lot needs replacing, make sure you know where you can buy new bits.

- Check the frame and forks for obvious dents or cracks, or to see if bits have been welded together. These are the most expensive parts to replace, so if you notice a problem, move on.
- If the frame isn't the right size for you, there's no point buying it.
- Look to see if the wheels are buckled or if there are many spokes missing. Lift the bike up and spin the wheels. If they wobble about a lot, they could become a problem. Replacing both wheels plus tyres can easily cost £100.
- See if the brakes work. Are the cables frayed? Are the brake pads worn down (i.e. can you no longer see the ridges in the pads?)? This is a relatively cheap fix, so if everything else about the bike is OK, this isn't a deal breaker.
- Check the chain isn't rusty or baggy.
- Look at the sprockets (cogs on the back wheel) and the chain rings (cogs on the front, by the pedals). If they are in good condition, their teeth will be sharp, pointy and evenly spaced. If they have become rounded, you won't be able to change gears smoothly and you'll need to buy a new chain, chain ring, and cassette (collection of sprockets/cogs on the back wheel), which will cost around £50.

MAKING SURE YOUR BIKE FITS

Never buy a bike that doesn't fit you – it will be uncomfortable to ride and can cause all sorts of aches and pains in knees, bottoms and backs.

- Straddle the frame. If there is a crossbar, the bar should not be more than 1.5 inches away from your crotch with road bikes and hybrids, and at least 2 inches away on mountain bikes.
- Your arms should be sloping forward to reach the handlebars, but not stretched.
- You should be able to reach the brakes and gears easily, without straining.
- When pedalling, your legs and knees should never feel overstretched or too scrunched up.
- Sitting on the saddle, you should be able to touch the floor when on your tiptoes.
- If you have found the right frame size, you can adjust the saddle and handlebar height using an Allen key or by unscrewing a bolt. If you have to have either as high or low as they can go, try going up or down a frame size.

OFF YOU GO!

Well, there you have it. Hopefully, the bike-buying process is now demystified and you can buy the perfect bike for you – not too big, not too small, within your budget and capable of everything you need it to do. Now you just need to go and buy it – a happy, happy day. Riding home on a new bike for the first time is a wonderful thing. The other day, I saw a girl on a gleaming new machine gingerly riding away from a bike shop in London with a huge smile on her face. She looked as nervous as a first-time mum driving home from the hospital with her newborn in the back, and just as delighted. Just the way it should be. Enjoy it!

ACCESS-ORIZING YOU AND YOUR BIKE

OK. You've got wheels. Now you get to jazz them up. Before you do, though, a wallet warning: it is very easy to get carried away in bike shops and end up spending an absolute fortune on goodies you neither need nor want. It is worth bearing in mind there are only actually two accessories you absolutely cannot live without if you are using your bicycle in an everyday sort of way, and they are locks and lights.

But if you want to personalize your bike and avoid the ignominy of rolling into the bike shed and finding someone else astride the self-same model, it's never been easier. Some bike shops even offer so-called 'Pimp My Ride' services to customers wanting to tart up their bicycles, whether it's replacing a boring old silver chain with a purple one or stencilling the frame with the pin-up of the day. For the 2009 Tour de France, Lance Armstrong commissioned a number of big-name artists to spruce up some of his bikes – Damien Hirst stuck dead butterflies all over his creation and it later sold for $500,000 at an auction in New York.

But you don't need to be a multi-millionaire artist to make your bike look better. It's easy and cheap to upgrade your saddle, or swap pedestrian black tyres for those in a more interesting hue – Halo tyres come in most colours on the spectrum and are very puncture-resistant to boot. Incidentally, when buying a bike, particularly from an independent bike shop, it is always worth asking if they'll let you switch any of the easily removable components for bits you like more. My favourite quick switch is to redo the handlebar tape on my road bike. It only costs around £6 a go and is a simple but strangely satisfying job. If you know what you're doing, you can even respray the frame when you fancy a change. Amy Fleuriot, founder of the Cyclodelic bike fashion brand, has an all-gold bike she calls Lady Godiva.

It's not all about the look, of course. There is no point buying something that doesn't work or fit, whether it's a helmet that perches on top of your head like a mortarboard, or a white pannier that looks like it's been to Glastonbury if it goes anywhere near a puddle. This chapter will help you decide which accessories you need – or want – and which to leave for some other unfortunate to waste their money on.

THE ABSOLUTE ESSENTIALS

LIGHTS

Unless you are certain you will never cycle in the dark, or even at dusk or in bad weather, you'll be needing a front and back light. Only Dutch bikes tend to come with lights already fitted, often using a dynamo system which powers the bulb as you pedal or as the wheels turn. Usually, though, you'll have to buy your own set.

For city cycling, the main aim is for other people to see you, rather than for your lights to illuminate the road ahead, so you don't necessarily need a torch-like beam. Bright LEDs will do. Don't buy really cheap ones, though, as they tend to eat batteries. Expect to spend at least £15 per light. Beware, too, of those that take annoying-sized, expensive batteries you can't buy in a multi-pack, and always check on the packaging to see the run time. Good ones will see you all the way through the winter; lousy ones will barely last a weekend. The best lights allow you to be seen at an angle as well as straight on, so look for ones that don't just shine in front – you'll be able to tell this by looking to see if the clear bit housing the LED curves around the side.

If you are going to be doing a lot of cycling down dark country lanes, you'll have to splash quite a bit more cash for a strong front light – these are bigger and bulkier than city lights and tend to cost £40 upwards.

Lights almost always come with a bracket to fix to your handlebars and seat stem. Annoyingly, every time a manufacturer upgrades a light, they tend to make a slightly different bracket, so if some sod nicks one of your lights (an infuriatingly frequent occurrence), expect to have to fit a new bracket. If you have a rear rack regularly piled high with parcels and the like, thus obscuring your back light, you'll need to buy an extra bracket that attaches to the back of the rack.

You can get fined £30 for not having lights, though the government has finally changed the silly law that previously made flashing back lights illegal.

A GOOD LOCK

Maybe even two, if you live somewhere rough and you have a quick-release front tyre. Don't scrimp on a lock, even if you have a naff bike. The more you pay, the better it will be.

In an ideal world, you'll get a D-lock to secure your back wheel and frame to something solid, and a cable lock to loop through your front wheel and other nickable bits.

See chapter 6 for more on choosing the right lock as well as the lowdown on how to keep your bike yours.

OTHER RECOMMENDED ACCESSORIES

A TRACK PUMP
(AKA STANDING PUMP)

This may sound like a superfluous indulgence that will clutter up your hallway and irritate anyone you live with, but believe me when I tell you that one of these will make your life better. They don't cost more than about twenty quid, but they are the best way of getting your tyres pumped up properly. They're also fun to use – I sometimes imagine myself detonating a particularly ugly building when pressing down on the handle of mine.

A poxy little hand pump simply doesn't do the trick, other than to inflate your tyres enough to get home after repairing a puncture. Buy one with a pressure gauge so you can check if you've put in the right amount of air. Look on your tyres for a number in front of the letters PSI to see how high you need to go (PSI is simply a unit of pressure, and stands for 'pounds per square inch').

One of the most common errors people make is not pumping their tyres up to anything like the correct pressure. When you press your tyre on the side, it should be rock solid (mountain bike tyres excepted). My dear friend Lexy couldn't understand why riding her hybrid had become such a trial until she went into a bike shop and the man told her that her tyres were at 10PSI, when they were supposed to be at 120PSI. It felt like a different bike when she rode home. To learn once and for all how to pump your tyres up properly, see p. 114.

MUDGUARDS

If your bike doesn't come with these as standard, buy some. Unless you live in some mysteriously rainless pocket of the planet, you will at some point get rained on as you cycle, and you'll get a whole lot wetter and grubbier without mudguards ('fenders' to Americans).

There's a strange view among the serious biking fraternity that fitting mudguards is somehow an insult to the bicycle, that it spoils the aesthetics and makes you look like an amateur. These people are fools, and they're the ones whose trousers get splattered with dirty puddle water in bad weather.

You can either fit full, permanent mudguards, which are bolted to your bike and so are secure but a pain to take on and off. Or you could go for the halfway house of 'racing' mudguards, which attach to the frame with durable rubber straps and can be easily whipped off in fine weather. I've seen Lance Armstrong with a set of these fitted to his zillion pound Trek, and if they're good enough for the seven-times Tour de France winner, they're good enough for me.

For mountain bikes, you may just want a back guard which attaches to your seat post and sits higher above your back wheel than ordinary ones, though these are not terribly effective at keeping you dry (they mostly just repel big clumps of mud).

If you want to fit mudguards to your bike, check that there is enough clearance between the front wheel and the frame. On bikes with particularly compact geometry, the front wheel is sometimes too close to fit a guard, as it will catch your toe when you turn a sharp corner.

One last thing: some mudguards don't come with the nuts and bolts you need in order to attach them to your bike. Check before you leave the shop that you have what you need. Better still, coax them into fitting them for you. Be nice, and they'll usually oblige.

CHAIN GUARD

This is a plastic or metal casing which seals your chain and gear cogs away so you don't get oily legs. It also stops the chain from getting dirty or rusty and so needs degreasing and lubricating far less often. It is not possible to fit a guard on all bikes, as some can stop derailleurs from functioning properly, so check before you buy.

A BELL

All new bikes these days are legally supposed to come with a bell attached, but if yours doesn't, buy one. The jury's out on whether it's more polite to shout 'Excuse me!' than ding your bell when a pedestrian has meandered into a bike lane (see p148), but it is always good to have the option.

SKIRT/COAT GUARD

This is a device which fits over your rear wheel to stop coats or skirts getting caught in the spokes. Again, not all bikes can take these (you sometimes need fitted mudguards); they are far and away most common on Dutch bikes.

A BASIC TOOL KIT

Containing three tyre levers, a multi-tool and a spare inner tube. See chapter 4 for what to do with them.

SEAT PROTECTOR

You can buy these, but a trusty plastic bag or shower cap will also stop your seat getting wet when you lock it up outside.

OTHER ACCESSORIES YOU MIGHT FANCY

MIRRORS

Fit these to your handlebars or top tube if you really must, but don't think they're a substitute for actually turning around to look behind you. Communicating with other road users is one of the best ways not to get knocked off your bike, so that quick glance over your shoulder is essential, not just to see who's coming but also to tell whoever it is that you've seen them too.

A KICK STAND

Can't be fitted on all bikes, but handy when there's nothing to lean your bike up against (or you don't want to ruin the paintwork).

A BOTTLE CAGE

If you ever get thirsty while you ride, attach a bottle cage to your frame. They're rarely more than a fiver and will keep a bottle secure and within your grasp as you cycle. I once saw a Dutch bike with an integrated coffee cup holder, but I'll leave it up to you to decide whether that's a good idea.

A BIKE COMPUTER

Sounds dreadfully spoddy, but there is a certain geeky pleasure in knowing how fast you're going, what your average speed is, how many calories you've burned and how far you've cycled. You can buy a simple bike computer for £15, or you can buy one for an awful, awful lot more if you want it equipped with GPS technology, heart rate monitors and the like. They look like digital watches with no strap, and attach either to your handlebars or your handlebar stem. Most people agree that Garmin makes the best bike computers.

CLIPLESS PEDALS
(AKA STEP-IN PEDALS OR SPDS)

If you plan to cycle your bicycle far and/or fast on a regular basis, you could exchange your ordinary pedals for 'clipless' ones.

Though the name would suggest otherwise, these require you to clip special cycling shoes into the pedals. These shoes have plastic or metal cleats screwed into the underside. When you step into the pedal, a mechanism automatically grips on to the cleat, making a very satisfying click. Just as some people always refer to all vacuum cleaners as Hoovers, these pedals are sometimes called SPDs (Shimano Pedaling Dynamics), which is the brand name of the popular clipless system made by components manufacturer Shimano in the 1990s.

The advantage of this set-up is that a minimal amount of energy is wasted throughout the whole pedal revolution. This is particularly handy when going uphill, as even the up-strokes propel you onwards, and they stop your feet from slipping in bad weather too.

Getting used to this arrangement can take a little time, and prepare yourself for a few embarrassing moments at traffic lights where you can't quite release your foot from the cleat in time to stop, and keel over like a drunkard. When I got my first pair, aged twenty-eight, it was like learning to ride a bike

Everyone gets confused about why 'clipless' pedals are the ones you have to clip into, but 'clipless' simply refers to the absence of old fashioned toe-clips.

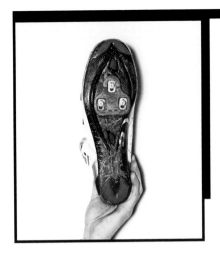

all over again, only with my boyfriend holding my steed steady, rather than my dad, as I got the hang of clipping in and out. Contrary to my fears, however, it really is not all that difficult. And bar a few bloodcurdling incidents in the early days when I forgot I was attached to the bike when stopping to look at the map, I've never looked back.

The main disadvantage is that, once you've fitted these pedals, you can't really cycle in normal shoes. And given that you can't walk any distance in cleated shoes (they often have uneven soles, and the cleats will make you sound like a tapdancer as you walk), you'll always have to carry another pair to put on at the other end.

If you don't want to go the whole hog, you could get multi-purpose pedals. These only have a cleat grip mechanism on one side, so if you are wearing ordinary shoes, just flip them over and use the flat surface. They're a good option if you want to use your bike just to pop to the shops or to bike to work as well as to do long rides on the weekend. Bear in mind, though, that they do have a tendency to always flip round to the side you don't want, and the flat side isn't quite as comfortable to pedal in civilian shoes as ordinary pedals.

Whichever system you go for, make sure you get compatible shoes. You can adjust cleats to alter the amount of pressure needed to extricate yourself from the pedals. If you're commuting, you'll probably want to be able to get your foot out quickly and easily: look for cleats which offer an element of what is known as 'float', i.e., room for manoeuvre. Anyone racing or touring and not encountering traffic lights at every junction will prefer being clipped in more securely. It's worth getting someone from a bike shop to help you get set up with this – getting it wrong can result in knee problems. If you buy your pedals and shoes in the same place, the shop is usually happy to fix the cleats on for you.

For a discussion on the aesthetics of cycling shoes, see pp. 88 and 103.

AND NOW FOR THE GREAT HELMET DEBATE

If you want to wear one, do. If you don't, don't. Simple as that. There is no legal requirement in most countries. In the UK, you only have to wear one if you enter bike races or certain organized rides.

You really have to assess what you think is the actual risk of your head hitting the tarmac. Contrary to what the scaremongers would have you believe, cycling is not an inherently dangerous activity. Hospital admission statistics from the UK government show that while head injuries are the leading source of injury to both pedestrians and car occupants, cyclists are most likely to hurt their arms or shoulders (Road Casualties Great Britain: 2007. Department for Transport). So surely those who travel by car or foot should be the ones wearing helmets, rather than those using pedal power?

The truth is that wearing a helmet can only help you if you come off your bike. The pro helmet lobbyists will roll out all sorts of statistics and horror stories to persuade you of this fact. Few doctors or dentists would argue against them. Yet evidence suggests that while protecting your head is helpful if you simply fall off and bang your head on the way down, helmets will not necessarily save you if you find yourself in a high speed collision with a motor vehicle. Having seen photographs of cyclists who have had the misfortune of being hit at speed, and seen their helmets smashed to smithereens, I can believe it.

It is slightly different where children are concerned: not only do they have softer skulls, but they are far more likely to come off their bikes through youthful recklessness/exuberance. By that logic, however, helmets should be dished out at playtime, given the number of children who fall over and hit their heads tearing around the schoolyard at break. If I had a little one strapped on to my bike, I would get them a helmet, though, as they couldn't easily react to a fall. In September 2009, the Association of Paediatric Emergency Medicine (APEM), which represents accident and emergency specialists in the UK, called on the government to make it illegal for children under sixteen to cycle without wearing head protection.

But in countries which have really embraced cycling, almost no one wears helmets, including children and toddlers. In Holland, for example, where 27 per cent of journeys are made by bicycle (compared to 1 per cent in the UK), just 3 per cent of cyclists bother. Of course, the Netherlands has an extremely bike-friendly infrastructure, with an extensive network of cycle lanes which are totally segregated from traffic, but it is interesting nonetheless.

There have also been studies suggesting that helmet wearers take more risks than those without, and that motorists overtake them with less care (see for example Dr Ian Walker's research at the University of Bath). No one has ever really proved that helmet wearing reduces casualty rates either. What has been proved,

Nowadays there is a huge variety of helmets on the market, from those disguised as ordinary hats, to round, hard shell helmets like those worn by skaters and snowboarders.

however, is that where helmets are made compulsory, such as in parts of Australia, cycling rates go down. Couple that with the fact that cycling gets safer the more cyclists there are, and you have the argument that helmet wearing should definitely not be made law.

I wear a helmet on the occasions when I think I am more at risk of hurting myself – i.e., in wet weather, when the roads are slippery, or when I'm going for a long ride and will be travelling fast. Or if I'm doing a triathlon or sportive (see p. 228) and won't be allowed to compete without it. The reasons I don't bother half the time can be summed up like this: I believe the risk to me is far outweighed by the joy I will feel at having the wind in my hair, and the convenience of not having to lug around a helmet at my destination – it is such a pain cycling to the shops and trying to juggle a basket with a helmet and anything else I'm carrying. Whenever someone berates me for cycling without a helmet, I always wonder whether they regularly do enjoyable/convenient things that could, in some unlikely scenario, kill them – drink too much, overeat, speed, jaywalk . . .

I've fallen off my bike twice in ten years. Once, when I was stupid enough to try and cycle after a massive snowfall, and another time when I hit a patch of black ice. On neither occasion did I hit my head. My boyfriend, however, also hit some ice one morning, went over his handlebars and hit his helmeted head. The helmet cracked; his skull didn't. Make of that what you will.

If you find the idea of wearing a plastic safety hat so abhorrent that it puts you off cycling, don't wear one. Instead, do everything you can to cycle safely and enjoy yourself (see chapter 5).

For more information on helmet efficiency, see:

ANTI COMPULSORY HELMET WEARING

- ↘ The Bicycle Helmet Research Foundation:
  http://www.cyclehelmets.org
- ↘ Search for 'helmets' on the website of the CTC,
  the national cyclists' organization:
  www.ctc.org.uk

PRO COMPULSORY HELMET WEARING

- ↘ The Bicycle Helmet Safety Institute, a US-based helmet
  advocacy programme:
  http://www.bhsi.org
- ↘ The Safety is Sexy campaign:
  http://safetyissexy.blogspot.com

HOW TO FIND THE RIGHT HELMET

But if you do want to wear one, don't despair, as helmet design has improved massively in recent years. My first helmet, in the eighties, was fluorescent pink, made out of polystyrene and was around about the size of those dryers old ladies sit under when getting their perms set.

There are two main kinds of helmets – light, aerodynamic, almond-shaped ones with loads of air vents, such as the ones they wear on the Tour de France; and round, hard shell ones similar to the type skateboarders and snowboarders sport.

Generally, the more expensive the helmet, the lighter and better ventilated it will be. Paying more will not get you a safer helmet, however. Anything with the European voluntary safety standard CE EN 1078 should be fine – you don't need to pay more than a tenner if you go to Argos.

Helmets made by Bern seem to suit almost everyone, but they and other hard shell hats aren't really suitable for long rides, as they lack ventilation and you'll get a horribly sweaty head. Plus they are often quite heavy and can make the wearer look like a First World War soldier – a boon or a bind, depending on your view. For everyday cycling, I have the Bern 'Muse' helmet, which has no air vents at all, but which is good for keeping hair dry in the rain. Apparently, I look as though I am off to Pony Club when I have it on, which I rather like, as I was denied riding lessons as a child. When I'm doing longer rides, I prefer a sportier, lighter, better ventilated design. I think Giro does the nicest ones, though they are often criminally expensive.

You can buy women-specific helmets, but generally this just means they come in smaller sizes or in pastel colours. I have a women's Giro in gold, which fits me far better than the unisex models. Sawaka Faruno makes stylish models for women, decorated with pretty designs.

Helmet designers are becoming increasingly creative – Bobbin Bicycles sells a Mr Ben bowler hat helmet in black felt, inspired by the classic kids' cartoon. Danish-designed Yakkay helmets come with a range of stylish covers which disguise a boring old helmet as a baseball cap, sun hat or furry Russian hat. Dahon, best known for its folding bikes, has developed a folding helmet called the Pango, which folds to half the size of a regular helmet – shame it makes you look like a Power Ranger.

There is no point wearing a helmet that doesn't fit you. As a general rule, if it doesn't feel snug as soon as you put it on, it doesn't fit and you should try a different size or model. The exception here are helmets which require you to stick little cushioned pads into the shell until you get the right fit, such as the Yakkays. A helmet should not wobble around on your head, and if you push up the front of the helmet with one finger, it shouldn't slide off your forehead. The straps should be as tight as possible without hurting your chin. The helmet should sit nicely, with the front rim or visor horizontal. Don't wear your helmet like a bonnet: if the front is further back than your hairline, pull it forward.

SOME HELMETS TO INVESTIGATE ARE:
- **Bell:** www.bellbikehelmets.com
- **Bern:** www.bernunlimited.com
- **Giro:** www.giro.com
- **Lazer:** www.lazerhelmets.com
- **Nutcase:** www.nutcasehelmets.com
- **Pro-tec:** http://pro-tec.net
- **Sawaka Faruno:** www.cyclefashion.co.uk
- **Yakkay:** www.yakkay.com

CARRYING STUFF

Unless you're only going to use your bike for sport, you'll have to cart things about when you cycle. If you don't like the idea of a cumbersome messenger bag, or don't fancy the sweaty back syndrome with a rucksack, consider fitting a basket and/or luggage rack(s) to your bicycle. Note that owners of folding bikes often have to buy bags and racks designed specifically for use with their model.

BACK RACKS

Many bikes can take at least a back rack – check that there are the necessary bosses (holes) to affix one. You're looking at about £35 for an ordinary, lightweight aluminium model. If you are going to be carrying crazy loads you'll need a stronger, more expensive steel one. Prepare yourself for a bit of a battle attaching the rack the first time – you may have to bend it to make it fit. Once you get the hang of it, you can take a rack off in minutes, so you're by no means stuck with it for ever and always.

If you don't have the bosses, you'll need a special rack that attaches to the seat post, though these can't carry as much weight.

Bike snobs tend to object violently to racks on the basis that they don't look cool and spoil the geometry of the bike. There is an element of truth in this, but they aren't half handy. As well as carrying stuff, a back rack doubles up as a mudguard.

If you have a rear rack, spend a few pounds on some bungee cords to secure unusual shaped objects to the rack. Even better, get a cargo net, which is one of the most useful things I have ever bought for my bike – it's just an elasticated web with plastic hooks on the side, but is brilliant for securing shopping bags and odd-shaped parcels.

FRONT RACKS

You only really need these if you're planning a big adventure and are carrying a ton of stuff. Front racks are either mounted low on the front fork or on the handlebars; both can sometimes mess with the steering and are not always suitable for bikes with front suspension or drop handlebars.

PANNIERS

These bags usually come in pairs and attach to the rack either via straps or clips. Sometimes, the pair are joined together and you just sling them over the rack. It's worth looking out for designs with carrying straps, as it's a huge pain lugging them about otherwise.

Some panniers look like shopping bags; others like rucksacks. In both of these, the clip is usually hidden behind a padded pocket so as not to get in the way when used off the bike.

If you're looking for a heavy-duty, all-weather pannier, you can't get better than Ortleib, made out of a tarpaulin-type material. No one I know who has invested in these German-made bags has a bad word to say about them. They really do not let in any water. I have a polka-dot pannier made by another German manufacturer, Haberland, which I'd recommend to anyone looking for something a bit less butch. Other panniers are not made from a waterproof material but include a rain cover which fits over the top of the bag in poor weather.

Beware of panniers which only close using Velcro or magnets. I bought a very pretty turquoise shopping bag pannier which only shuts when it is almost empty.

BAR BAGS

These are little knapsacks which attach to your handlebars and are usually designed so that you can access them easily while you're riding. They don't hold much, but are useful for stashing maps, your mobile and an emergency chocolate bar on a long ride.

BASKETS

The demure way to schlep goods by bicycle. Most hook on to handlebars or front racks – you need wide handlebars for this. You can get them in traditional wicker or more modern metal. Bicycles with baskets rarely get stolen, apparently – I once asked someone from a cycle insurance company why, and he said, 'Cos even bike thieves have street cred.'

SADDLEBAGS

These tuck under your saddle and are attached by straps and/or a plastic holster connected to the underside of the seat. They are handy for keeping your tool kit and spare inner tube, but not much else.

BRANDS TO INVESTIGATE INCLUDE:

↘ **Arkel (Canadian):** www.arkel-od.com

↘ **Banjo Brothers (American):** www.banjobrothers.com

↘ **Basil (Dutch):** www.basil.nl

↘ **Bici Concepts (American):** www.biciconcepts.com

↘ **Carradice (British):** www.carradice.co.uk

↘ **Cordo (Dutch):** www.cordo.com

↘ **Cyclodelic (British):** www.cyclodelic.co.uk

↘ **Gilles Berthoud (French):** www.gillesberthoud.fr/anglais

↘ **Haberland (German):** www.haberland.de (site is in German)

↘ **Knog (Australian):** www.knog.com.au

↘ **Minnehaha (American):** www.minnehahabags.com

↘ **Nari/Furi (Japanese):** www.narifuri.com

↘ **Ortlieb (German):** www.ortlieb.com

↘ **Zwei (German):** www.zwei.de

CHILD SEATS

If you want to transport your child by bicycle, you can. Ignore scaremongers who accuse you of being reckless – most babies and children love being on a bike and, with the right kit, you can transport them safely. Note that not all bikes are suitable for carrying children. Road bikes tend to be the least child-friendly, and for some systems you need a crossbar and cannot have drop handlebars.

As long as your child is old enough to hold his or her head up unaided, you can give it a go. Bike seats generally start from age nine months upwards, and can be attached to the front or back of the bike. Front seats are best for littlest ones – the parent has a view of the child (and can see if they're nodding off and their head starts rolling round), and the child has a view of the open road, which they find enormously exciting. When children get beyond a certain weight (usually 18kg/40lb), they need to sit on the back. Don't let your children carry anything when strapped in – if they drop a mitten or even a biscuit, it could get caught in the spokes.

Having a seat plus child plonked on your bike will change the way it rides, so practise somewhere safe and quiet, ideally with an inanimate object doubling up for your child in the seat. You will find the bike more difficult to steer and manoeuvre and it will feel very top heavy, but it is fine once you get used to it. The biggest issue most parents face when transporting their offspring by bike is getting the child on and off the bike, so be very careful to hold the bike steady during the process. A kick stand can help, but don't rely on it.

BOBIKE

↘ This Dutch brand makes well regarded seats for children aged nine months to ten years:
www.bobike.nl

HAMAX

↘ Makes a reclinable baby seat called the Sleepy, which can be mounted on bikes with or without a luggage rack:
www.hamax.com

WEERIDE

↘ The WeeRide Kangaroo is a popular bike seat for children aged between one and five, and is mounted on the crossbar:
www.weerideuk.co.uk

TRAILERS, WAGONS AND CARGO BIKES

If you have more than one child, look into bike trailers and wagons to tow behind your bike, or cargo bikes, which come with a wagon attached. The advantage of a trailer over a bike seat is that it is more stable and affects the handling of the bike far less, though they will slow you down. They can also carry much heavier children, and many have a cover to keep them dry. Little ones love feeling regal as they sit back in comfort, and tend to enjoy the attention they receive from people they pass. If the trailer is very low down, consider fitting a flag at the height of your saddle to make sure motorists can see it. Only buy one if you're sure you'll use it a lot, as they are initially very expensive (£1,000-plus).

Here are a few options to start you off:

TAGA

↘ A bike and pushchair rolled into one:
www.taga.nl

TRIOBIKE

↘ This is a futuristic-looking pushchair which attaches to the front of a special bike. Two children can sit in comfy seats, securely strapped in with safety belts. The bike can easily be detached for when the children are at nursery:
www.triobike.co.uk

XTRA CYCLES

↘ These are customizable bikes that can take bike seats, trailers and more:
www.xtracycle.com

BAKFIETS

↘ Dutch company selling a wide range of cargo bikes:
www.bakfiets.nl/eng/

CHRISTIANIA BIKES

↘ Danish company specializing in cargo bikes:
www.christianiabikes.com

TAG-A-LONG TRAILER BIKES

↘ When children get too big for a child seat or trailer, you could hook on a third-wheel 'tag-a-long' cycle to your bike, which allows the child to help you pedal or simply sit back and enjoy the ride. You just hitch the trailer to a rear luggage rack on your bike, adjust the saddle and handlebars to the right height and off you both go.

Cycling hero: Josie Dew

For many parents, even the thought of cycling to the shops with a child on the back of the bike is too much. But Josie Dew towed her two-year-old daughter Molly over 10,000 miles around England in a bike trailer and has lived to tell the tale.

A fearless adventurer, Josie has written seven books about her life in the saddle. She started cycle touring aged eleven, exploring Wales, the Lake District and Scotland on two wheels, as well as cycling the 20 mile round trip to school every day. At fifteen, she set up her own catering company, cooking and delivering three-course meals by bicycle and cycle trailer, and then set off on a lifetime adventure seeing the world by bike.

She has ridden from Vancouver all the way down the west coast of the USA and on through Mexico's Baja peninsula; across the Himalayas, around New Zealand, Iceland and Japan, and other countries too numerous to mention.

She continued cycling all the way through her pregnancy in 2006, and gave birth to her daughter just after returning home from a bike ride. Halfway through 2007, Molly completed her first 1,500 miles strapped to the back of her mother's bike. In 2008, Josie married her builder, and the happy couple spent their honeymoon – what else? – cycling around the Isle of Wight.
www.josiedew.co.uk

CYCLE
CHIC

If there is one thing, after safety, that deters many a right-thinking person from becoming a cyclist, it is the fear of looking like one. Why would anyone with even a smidgen of style sense and just a hint of self-respect want to join a gang with a uniform that encompasses both Lycra and luminous yellow?

The biking fraternity has long conspired to make cycling seem difficult and technical, encouraging the idea that to ride a bicycle you have to divorce yourself from the norms of society. (This is why some bike shop employees have no social skills.) A sort of sartorial masochism has long reigned, suggesting that Proper Cyclists must suffer not only on the hills, but also in the style stakes.

This is tosh. You do not need to embrace spandex in order to cycle. If you would never normally venture out in anything that was in danger of hugging your figure, now is not the time to start. For short jaunts, at least, you can wear your ordinary clothes, in ordinary fabrics, and don't let anyone tell you otherwise. You know yourself which outfits won't get caught in the chain and which don't have enough ventilation to keep things fresh. Billowing trousers are better left at home unless tamed with some cycle clips. And it is difficult to maintain dignity pedalling in a pencil skirt. There is no point stubbornly cycling in anything which is likely to split or tear, especially when those outfits can simply be saved for the days the bike stays in the shed. If you're the sort of person who breaks into a sweat just putting the kettle on, you'll just have to get changed at the other end.

Of course, cycling specific clothing has its place. If you're regularly riding more than a few miles at a time, you may well want to investigate proper cycling kit – a jersey with big pockets on the back to stash flapjack and a map on a long ride, padded pants to stave off saddle sores and merino wool vests to keep you warm but sweat-free in the winter months. The happy news is that all this stuff is becoming less hideous by the week, as designers finally cotton on to the radical idea that not all cyclists want to look like perverted glow-in-the-dark numpties.

But don't be conned into thinking you have to invest in any special gear. Everything you need to wear on a bicycle is already in your wardrobe – if you don't believe me, take a look at the wonderful www.copenhagencyclechic.com blog, which coined the phrase 'Cycle Chic', if such a phrase is indeed coinable. See if you can spot one person pedalling around the streets of the Danish capital wearing Lycra – or a helmet for that matter. Partly thanks to Copenhagen Cycle Chic, a whole fashion scene has developed around people who want to look stylish on their bicycles.

If you are prepared to cycle slowly enough so as not to sweat offensively – and to fit mudguards and, ideally, a chain guard to your bike (see p. 63) – even your gladdest rags can get to the end of a short ride intact, oil free and smelling fresh. Don't think you have to be too sensible, either. At the end of Some Like It Hot, Marilyn Monroe pedals down to the seafront in a floor-length ballgown and heels, to no ill effect. Tony Curtis and Jack Lemmon manage just fine in natty suits too. And anyone who has seen Dame Vivienne Westwood bombing around south London in one of her more otherworldly ensembles can testify that cycling and the more outré end of high fashion can and do mix. While it isn't the cleverest idea to wear all black on a night ride, resist the notion that a fluorescent tabard, cagoule or sash is a must. Cycling safely is far more important.

There are, in my tolerant mind, only two Cycling Don'ts when wearing civilian gear on a bike. They are the Bum Crack Reveal and the Lower Back Exposé, two occupational hazards for anyone cycling in low-rise trousers and a too-short top. This is predominantly a female problem, though I've been stuck behind enough hipster boys in dire need of a belt to extend this warning to men as well. Avoiding BCR and LBE is easy – just wear long tops. While we're here: Ladies, remember that everyone can see your cleavage when you're hunched over your handlebars like that. And men: if you must wear Lycra, for goodness sake don't sit with your legs wide open. A confident man does not need to flaunt the contents of his cycling shorts.

FOR HER

For the perfect women's cycling outfit, I look to the beautiful American actress Jean Seberg in Jean-Luc Godard's *Breathless* (*À bout de souffle*). Though Seberg doesn't even go near a bicycle in the 1959 French film, everything she wears would transfer perfectly from the screen to the saddle.

Seberg's most iconic get-up comes from her first scene, where she is selling newspapers in a fitted T-shirt advertising the *New York Herald Tribune* and a pair of black cigarette pants that end just above her ankles. On her feet, she is wearing dark pumps. Had she and her caddish co-star decided to go on the run on bicycles instead of in a succession of stolen cars, they might never have got caught. The tapered trousers would clear the chain without getting dirty, the top would be comfy and airy enough to cycle fast without becoming too sweaty too quickly. She could maintain a good steady cadence in those practical shoes. Seberg, of course, also has perfect cycling hair. That gamine crop could withstand wind and sweat – and even a cycle helmet. More on avoiding 'helmet hair' later.

Equally perfect is the striped dress she wears to her first press conference as a rookie reporter. It has short sleeves and a collar, and is nipped in at the waist before flaring out into a full circle skirt to just past the knee – exactly the length and style to give the lady cyclist freedom of movement without flashing her knickers to the traffic.

While we're on a film tip, anything the girls in *Grease* wear will work a treat too. Capri pants aren't also called pedal-pushers for nothing, and knee-length prom dresses are great for cycling because they flare out enough not to restrict movement while being long enough to preserve your modesty. If you're brave enough to ape Olivia Newton-John's bad girl look at the end of the film, go right ahead. There's no way those spray-on trousers will get caught in the chain, but your crotch might welcome a little more breathing space on a long ride.

CAN YOU CYCLE IN HIGH HEELS?

Yes. If you have ordinary pedals, you can cycle in whatever footwear you like. That's not to say it's always a good idea, but you'll no doubt manage it.

It is perfectly possible to cycle in high heels. I find it much easier to cycle in a heel than to walk in one, and spend most winters razzing about town on my racing bike in a pair of knee high boots that make me two inches taller than I really am. But it's not always the cleverest thing to do, mostly because the soles tend to be very slippery and your feet are liable to slide right off the pedals as you push down.

Also, because you exert a lot more pressure than normal on the middle of the shoe, they can get ruined quite easily. Plus strapless heels might fall off when at an angle, which is bad news – cycling in bare feet hurts, and new shoes are expensive. I have a friend who lost one court shoe while navigating a particularly perilous gyratory system in London. The traffic was moving too fast to retrieve it, so she had to pedal to the pavement with one bare foot and then watch with dismay as a truck ran right over her shoe. Flip-flops tend not to stay on properly either, and the soles can bend mid-revolution, which is problematic. Sandals are fine, as long as the sole isn't too flimsy and they'll stay put on your feet.

If you're one of those people who cannot be seen in flats, I recommend wedges for cycling. I have a pair of polka-dot wedge sandals which I wear all through the summer, on and off the bike. Because they are a lot more solid than heels, you can press down harder on them and go far faster without destroying them. At the time of writing, London-based designer and bike fiend Anna Glowinski of Ana Nichoola was working on a range of high-heeled cycling shoes based on wedges, which I am eagerly awaiting.

The perfect cycling shoe has a sturdy sole. All the energy you create when pedalling is transmitted through your shoes, so if the soles are too soft or your feet are moving around, you are wasting effort. Buckles or Velcro are always preferable to laces, which can lead to hairy moments if they get caught up in the chain. If you have to wear laced shoes, make sure the laces are short and tucked in where possible.

FOR HIM

Male cyclists didn't always squeeze themselves into shorts that shrinkwrap their reproductive organs. Before DuPont chemist Joseph Shivers invented spandex, back in 1959, Tour de France cyclists dressed like international playboys, with film star sunglasses, sharp suits and fabulous knitwear. Pee-wee Herman might have been a joke character, but he knew how to rock a suit and bow tie on a bicycle.

As long as you are prepared to cycle gently and can negotiate a deal with a dry cleaner, there is no reason not to dress smartly in the saddle. You'll definitely need cycle clips to avoid oil stains, or long enough socks to tuck your trouser legs in. Don't wear a rucksack over the top, else you'll crumple the jacket – a look only Boris Johnson seems to find increases his popularity. If you want something made for the job, Dashing Tweeds, the London tailor, has designed a three-piece cycling suit, which includes well-concealed fastenings at the knee to transform ordinary suit trousers into plus-fours, as well as a discreetly reflective weave. Another tailor, Timothy Edwards, recently collaborated with the bike brand Rapha to create a bespoke cycling suit, which cost a heart-stopping £3,500. Paul Smith, who wanted to be a professional bike rider before turning to fashion, regularly includes bike-friendly gear in his collections too.

Some of Britain's most sartorially minded cyclists belong to the Tweed Cycling Club, a collection of anachronistic dandies who hark back to the days before Lycra and luminosity became the norm. The club's website explains their ethos:

For today's cyclist, skin tight Lycra may promise a reduction in wind resistance but also in decorum. A reflective yellow vest guarantees high visibility, but who would wish to be seen in such a garment? Certainly not the members of the Tweed Cycling Club. The Club's wheelmen and ladymembers wish for a return to the honest virtues of lugged steel, dynamo lighting and canvas saddlebags. A stout pair of plus fours offer day-long comfort while a Fair Isle vest takes the chill out of a frosty spring morning. As the Club passes the village green, a jaunty cap is doffed. The only performance enhancements are warm beer and Woodbines.

The club's founder, Jack Thurston, who also presents *The Bike Show* on Resonance FM, points out that even the pros used to dress well, and with imagination. 'There are some great photos of Il Campionissimo Fausto Coppi in the 1950s wearing great ballooning golfing trousers and argyle socks, a turtleneck jersey and Ray Ban sunglasses,' he says of the Italian Tour de France legend. Look on the club's website to see what their members wear on their sporadic Tweed Run rides: www.tweed.cc.

SHOULD I GET CYCLE CLIPS OR JUST ROLL UP A LEG?

Totally up to you. Whichever you choose, remember to revert to normal at your destination. I remember a very serious morning conference at the newspaper where I work, when one of the most eminent writers held forth at length on the Israel/Palestine conflict while standing with one leg of his suit rolled up. Not just that, but he was still wearing his fluorescent yellow sash.

WHY PADDED PANTS ARE YOUR BEST FRIEND

There are few garments more unattractive than a pair of Lycra padded cycling shorts. Not only do they stop at just the least flattering leg-truncating spot, but the spongy insert is all too reminiscent of a bulky sanitary towel from the pre-'Wings' era, as Tim Moore noted in his marvellous cycling travelogue, *French Revolutions*. No one, male or female, looks good in slinky cycling shorts. I know this to be true, having once attended that most oxymoronic of events, a Cycling Fashion Show, and seen what they do to even the pertest of bottoms.

Despite this, I am a committed fan – albeit often in secret. In the summer months, I often wear a pair under a pretty summer dress to disappoint perverts at traffic lights. Without taking this precaution, not only are you at risk of giving your fellow road users the sort of up-skirt shot paparazzi photographers pay their mortgages with, but you may experience some nasty chafing while you're at it. Men can do the same, and disguise the Lycra with ordinary shorts or trousers, though be careful the seams don't rub. Go for a long ride with an unpadded butt and you will not just have a sore behind but one riddled with saddle sores. You'll get unhygienically sweaty too.

I recently invested in a pair of Craft Bike Boxers, which look like hot pants but are actually a highly breathable pair of bike shorts with integrated anti-bacterial padding. I would never, ever wear them on their own (sore thighs! loss of dignity!), but the whole point is that you can slip them underneath ordinary trousers or skirts and feel the benefit without anyone else knowing your kinky secret. Men should never cycle any distance in baggy boxer shorts. Even if you are one of those blokes who likes things free and easy, you do not want any of your free and easy bits rubbing on the saddle.

If you want to wear shorts on their own, they need not be tight and made out of Lycra. Many baggy cycling shorts include padding too. These are usually marketed as mountain bike wear, but there's no reason you can't wear them on any old machine. Mountain bikers simply have a little more dignity than your average road rider, many of whom continue to labour under the misapprehension that Lycra looks good.

As well as baggies, both sexes can buy padded three-quarter-length trousers that are variously marketed as knickers (it's an American thing) or capris. These do make men look a bit girly, however, and have a tendency to stumpify women's legs. Nonetheless, I am very pleased with my Swrve capris, which are made with a water and wind repellent softshell exterior and a soft, warm bonded fleece inside and, brilliantly, look like ordinary pedal pushers. Very cosy for winter riding. See the end of the chapter for details of this and other brands, shops and designers.

Treat cycling shorts as an underwear substitute and wash them after every ride.

CAN YOU CYCLE IN JEANS?

For both sexes, jeans are only really suitable for shortish jaunts because of the seams in the crotch area. Attempting long distances in denim will cause great discomfort – the material is too stiff and unbreathable, and the seams will rub. Plus, of course, jeans are a disaster in the rain. You can, however, get cycling-specific jeans, which claim not to cause their wearer the same problems. Again, the US brand Swrve makes a pair which has a seamless, gusseted crotch, articulated knees, a lower front to stop a belt digging in with a slight rise in the back, and back pockets that fit a mini D-lock. An added bonus is the reflective strip on the inside of the right leg that is exposed when you turn up the jeans, keeping them out of the way of the chain and adding a good level of night-time visibility. New York make Osloh sells its own version too, as does the British brand Charge under the label Surface. Decide for yourself whether you'd be better saving your money and rolling up one leg of your ordinary pair, or simply putting your jeans on when you arrive.

DO CYCLING CAPS LOOK SILLY?

Yes – but in a good way. Tight little cycling caps are a throwback to the glory days of cycling, when Tour de France riders didn't have to wear helmets, would fill their water bottles with brandy and prepared for races by making love and eating freshly shot game. They are mostly just worn for fashion these days, particularly on the courier scene, but are also good for absorbing sweat. TWOnFRO, a London brand, makes very demure woollen caps for cyclists more concerned with style than sweat absorption. All caps do terrible things to hair, though, so if you wear one, you'll need to keep it on at your destination or head straight for a mirror on arrival.

STAYING CHIC
IN POOR WEATHER

Winter poses more of a sartorial challenge for cyclists. On the plus side, you'll sweat less, so you won't need to worry so much about turning up looking and smelling bad at the other end. But you'll have to contend with more frequent encounters with cycling's twin enemies: wind and rain. There are several approaches you can take here. You could become a fair weather cyclist, only wheeling out your bicycle when the meteorologists tell you it's safe to do so. Or you could buck up a bit and make a moderate investment in some rain gear, accepting a slight drop in the style stakes in order to arrive at your destination not looking like a drowned kitten. If there is a way of staying chic while cycling through a rainstorm, I have yet to discover it.

CAPES

Capes are making a comeback, and have the advantage of keeping you well ventilated but dry. The cheap synthetic ones will make you look as though you're cycling in a tent and can make arm signalling tricky, but if that doesn't bother you, go right ahead. Be careful with the really old-school ones which clip on to your bike, however, as they can be a bit dangerous.

A more stylish, and expensive, option would be to invest in a tailored cape, such as those lovingly sewn on Savile Row by Dashing Tweeds. This comes with a fairly hefty fashion warning: will this make you look like Miss Marple/ Sherlock Holmes? Is this a good thing? Annoyingly, it tends to be young, beautiful people who can carry off a tweed cape, while the rest of us look like Clarissa Dickson Wright going off to pluck some pheasants.

RAIN JACKETS

I opt for the less classy option of a cycle-specific cagoule, which has zips under the armpits to let air in or out, and a longer back to cover my bottom when I lean forward. Mine bundles up small so that I can carry it discreetly in my bag in the event of an unexpected shower.

My jacket is blue. I refuse to get a luminous one because a) they are horrible and you can't wear them to the pub without everyone thinking 'Who's the loser in the fluorescent cagoule?' and b) because I think there are other, equally effective ways of ensuring motorists see you – such as always looking behind you, signalling properly, and never getting so close to a vehicle that you can't see their mirrors. If a driver can't see you, it doesn't matter that your jacket makes you glow like a lump of phosphorus.

It is possible these days to get very swish cycling jackets that manage that rarest of feats: they don't look like bike gear. Here, men have the upper hand. The cult British brand Rapha makes much lusted-after 'softshell' jackets that combine functionality with high style. Softshell jackets are made from a technical woven material and let sweat out but stop the rain and wind from getting in. They are not totally waterproof but will keep you dry in a shower. In 2008, Rapha produced a limited edition of a hundred in a super-stylish Prince of Wales check, which managed to be windproof and water-resistant and had a handy rear pocket, zipped arm vents and discreet reflective piping. It sold out almost immediately, despite costing £450. Rapha keeps saying it might start making women's clothing, but I wouldn't hold your breath.

The Cyclodelic and Ana Nichoola women's ranges include a few cycling coats, and there are some beautiful cycling trenches sold by the French company Do You Velo? as well. Transport for London, weirdly, has introduced a cycling range under the label bspoke, which includes some boring but inoffensive khaki and black jackets for both sexes.

But you don't have to buy a special cycling coat. Just look out for a jacket which is cut low at the back so that it doesn't rise up when you lean forward, but which isn't so long that it's in danger of getting tangled in your spokes or dirtied by your chain. I wouldn't recommend anything with a hood, as it will obscure your view – unless you get a ridiculously close-fitting one, which will make you resemble a bobsled rider.

WATERPROOF TROUSERS

To keep your bottom half dry, you can avoid splashback from grimy puddles with mudguards, but if you really want to protect your legs you'll need to consider either full-on waterproof trousers – which look good on precisely no one, and will make you sweat like a boxer and rustle like a carrier bag. Or you could try newfangled 'Rain Legs' (www.rainlegs.co.uk), which are gaiters that attach to the front of your trousers or tights to protect your thighs. Rain Leg devotees swear they protect you from the worst of the wet and, because they are open at the back, they don't gather condensation and make you feel sweaty. You could also buy spats, which are cloth or leather gaiters covering the instep and ankle – www.cyclechic.co.uk sells them. They do look nasty, but bear in mind that, if it's bucketing it down, fewer people will be out in the streets to see your shameful outfit, and you can probably nip into the toilet on arrival to whip off your rain gear before any of your friends or colleagues excommunicate you for your style crimes.

HEADGEAR

You're going to get very cold ears cycling in the winter. You have various options here if you're wearing a helmet, including ear muffs, earwarming headbands and not particularly attractive tight fitting caps that cover your head underneath. If you're going helmetless, any warm hat will do, just make sure that any brims or flaps don't obscure your view when you turn your head. Buffs – multifunctional headgear you can wear as a scarf, bandana or headband – are good too.

BOOTIES

In winter, your feet will rapidly turn to ice on the bike. If you're doing more than a quick commute or trip to the shops, consider buying overshoes, which cyclists infantilize by referring to as 'booties'. These are generally made from wetsuit material or Lycra and look pretty stupid, but go on a long, cold ride without them and you'll be convinced your feet have fallen off. Overshoes have holes in the bottom to accommodate cycling shoes with cleats.

GLOVES

In winter, you will definitely need to wear gloves. Any with fingers will do, though you may find wool slips too much on your handlebars. I had some wool-lined leather ones that were just the ticket until I left them on a bench in Lancashire. I have cycled in mittens, and once resorted to putting my socks on my hands when I realized I'd left my gloves at home, but I wouldn't recommend it. If you're wondering why pro-cyclists wear fingerless gloves even in summer, it's less to do with keeping their hands warm and more to do with protecting them should they crash.

Cycling-specific gloves aren't always too revolting: I have a jaunty pair by the Australian brand Knog, which have L-O-V-E and H-A-T-E stitched across the knuckles. Proper cycling gloves have handy features, such as snug cuffs that stop your wrists getting chilly, and pads on the palms that protect the ulnar nerve area (the heel of the hand opposite the thumb). Generally, the more padding, the better. This is important if you don't want to develop 'handlebar palsy', an RSI-like condition caused by an inflammation of the nerve that runs along the entire length of the arm to the hand. This nerve becomes inflamed, usually either at the elbow or the wrist, when it has to absorb vibration and shock transmitted to the arm via the handlebars. You only need to worry about this if you're cycling a fair distance, however.

GROSS FACT: most cycling gloves include a cloth bit on the outside specifically designed for you to blow your nose on.

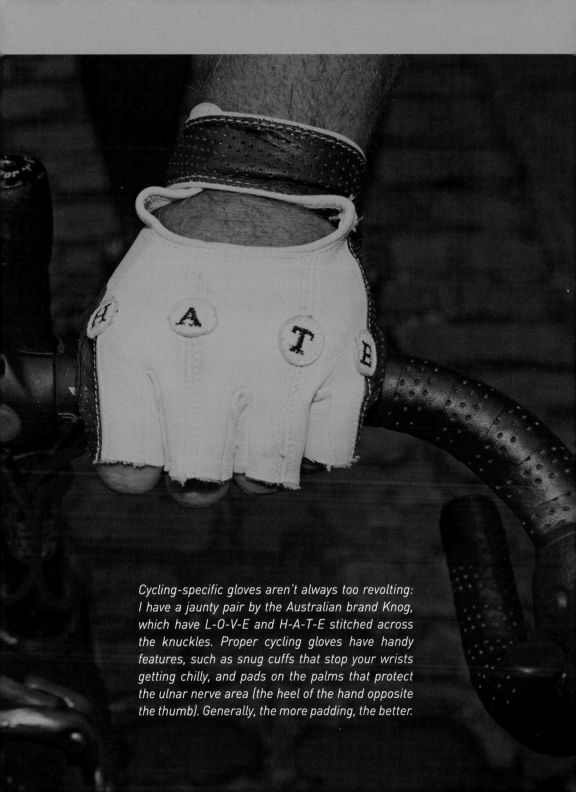

Cycling-specific gloves aren't always too revolting:
I have a jaunty pair by the Australian brand Knog,
which have L-O-V-E and H-A-T-E stitched across
the knuckles. Proper cycling gloves have handy
features, such as snug cuffs that stop your wrists
getting chilly, and pads on the palms that protect
the ulnar nerve area (the heel of the hand opposite
the thumb). Generally, the more padding, the better.

TECHNICAL GEAR: URGH

If you are planning on going fast and/or a long way, you will probably want to invest in some technical gear. Be warned: although things are rapidly improving, much of it is pretty awful. Women-specific gear is particularly woeful. As with so many goods aimed at women, far too much of it is pink, purple or a particularly girly turquoisy blue. For reasons I have yet to fathom, nothing ever seems to come in green.

Cycle clothing is generally so horrible because it is modelled on the garish gear worn by professional cyclists. Pro riders are essentially monomaniacal masochists who pride themselves on attempting ill-advised feats that mere mortals are sensible enough not even to consider – and the same goes for their colour combinations. Anyone who exercises free will to take part in races such as the Bordeaux–Paris, which begins at midnight and covers 575km with no stops, is not normal and really shouldn't be copied.

And yet, for a certain breed of male cyclist in particular, donning cycle clothing is all about pretending to be Lance Armstrong. Go on a bike ride any given Sunday, and you'll see streams of portly middle-aged men dressed like the Texan in the misguided hope that they may too one day wear the yellow jersey. All too often they are actually wearing a yellow jersey, which I find sweetly delusional.

The truth, of course, is that wearing proper cycling gear will in no way guarantee you pole position as the Tour rolls down the Champs-Élysées. The best bike clobber, however, will at least keep you dry and warm or cool, depending on the season. Despite objecting to 95 per cent of bike clothing, I own a whole drawerful of the stuff, which I either combine with ordinary clothes for comfort or practicality on short rides (such as the cycling shorts under a dress scenario) or don head to toe on longer expeditions.

If you're going on a proper bike ride, it's a good idea to layer up. Even in summer, you'll be surprised how cold you can suddenly get when waiting for your friends at the top of a big hill, or freewheeling down the other side.

A quick note on technical fabrics: their labels usually insist you wash them at 30 degrees with no fabric softener. I forget all the time and bung my cycling stuff in an ordinary 40 degree wash and have never had any problems.

BASE LAYER

Start with a base layer, i.e. a vest. These are often advertised with boasts of their 'wicking' abilities. This silly word is never used in ordinary life, but essentially means that the clever fabric moves sweat away from the skin to the outer surface of the garment, where it evaporates. A base layer should be tight-fitting and ideally made from that most cycle-friendly of natural materials, merino wool. Wool is naturally anti-bacterial, so your gear won't give off that deathly smell you get with polyester. It also wicks sweat better than any synthetic material, keeping you cooler and drier in the summer and warmer in cold weather. Bamboo fabric is good too. Cotton is not ideal, as it clings on to sweat and will become unpleasantly damp in next to no time. Like all cycling tops, a base layer should be low on the back to keep your kidneys warm (or your back protected from the sun) when you're leaning forward. An ordinary T-shirt will ride up, leaving your lower back, and possibly the top of your pants, exposed – a heinous look which, as previously discussed, all cyclists have a moral responsibility to avoid.

LEGGINGS, SHORTS AND TIGHTS

Then you'll want some shorts or leggings or tights. Men often prefer bib-type shorts with shoulder straps, ostensibly because they're more comfortable than ordinary shorts with a drawstring. They are undoubtedly good in the winter, because the high rise cut keeps your back and belly warm. They're a nightmare if you need the loo, though, and will make you look like a turn of the century strong man – a plus or negative depending on your view. Women tend not to wear bib shorts as much as men, mostly because the peeing problem is even more acute – though Gore Bike Wear had a patent pending on a pair of women's bib shorts with a special 'pee flap' at the time of writing.

JERSEYS AND GILETS

You'll also want some sort of top, ideally with a zip at least partway down the front for when you get too hot. Or a gilet – but I personally am allergic to those, largely because I associate them with horsey women who drive Land Rovers. Many cycling-specific tops include a handy back pocket for putting in your keys/phone/map/water bottle. For some irritating reason, women's jerseys often don't, or they incorporate a fiddly, hidden zipped pocket, which is difficult to access with one hand as you roll along. I love a roomy back pocket, because it means I don't need a pannier if I'm just going out for the day. Merino wool jerseys look classiest. I have one from the US brand Ibex which is marketed as a top for spinning classes indoors, but performs brilliantly in all weathers and looks acceptable off the bike too.

ARM WARMERS

Sounds like the most ridiculous thing ever – why not just put a jumper on? But actually, arm warmers (which look like long socks with no feet) are good for those awkward mid-season days when it's not quite worth putting on another layer but is a bit nippy for a short sleeved top. They're particularly useful if you're not carrying a bag, as you can just roll them up or stick them in your back pocket. Bolero cardigans are a decent civilian alternative.

LEG WARMERS

As above, but to bridge the gap between your shorts and socks.

CYCLING GLASSES

If you really want, you can buy special lightweight cycling sunglasses to keep dust and small insects out of your eyes, though they are very expensive and you'll look like Bono off the bike. I'd just stick with your ordinary shades.

COPING WITH HELMET HAIR

As with hats, so with helmets: put anything on your head for any length of time and it will probably mess with your hairdo. And according to an online survey commissioned by Cycling England in 2008, one in four women are too worried about helmets ruining their hair to ride their bikes. They didn't ask men, but no doubt there are vain enough blokes out there to be put off cycling for the same sad reason. It's pretty obvious what does and doesn't work here. Avoid anything that requires volume (spikes, quiffs, a beehive). Exercise caution with a fringe. If your hair isn't naturally straight but you would like it to be, accept that a helmet will leave it with ridges.

It is debatable what sort of helmet is kindest to hair. On the one hand, snowboarding helmets are best, as they are smooth, with few vents to imprint on your hair; on the other, the lack of vents will lead to a sweatier head. You can't win, I'm afraid.

WHY MIGHT I NEED PROPER CYCLING SHOES?

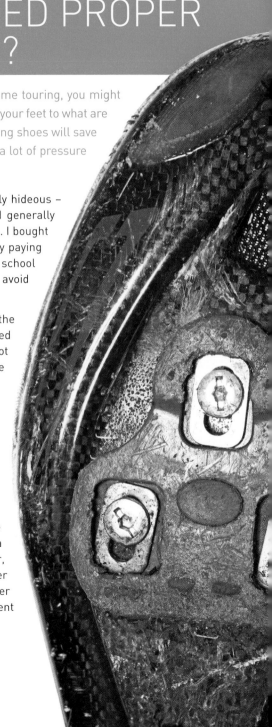

If you are planning on cycling for sport, or doing some touring, you might want to invest in some proper cycling shoes that clip your feet to what are confusingly named 'clipless' pedals (see p. 66). Cycling shoes will save your feet from hurting on a long ride, when you put a lot of pressure on the arch and ball of the foot.

I regret to inform you that these shoes are universally hideous – chunky to the point of looking remedial, clunky and generally available only in bafflingly vulgar colour combinations. I bought the nicest pair I could find, for the price I could justify paying (£60), and they still look like they belong on a primary school boy with rickets who can't yet tie his own laces. I try to avoid being seen in them unless actually on the bike.

If you don't want to get cleats, you could go for the halfway house of a sturdy cycling-specific shoe teamed with pedals with toe-clips or cages. These are not uniformly ugly – Quoc Pham makes some rather nice leather numbers – but you'd have a job fooling anyone into believing they are ordinary footwear.

The other option would be to get multi-purpose pedals which are flat on one side and with a cleat-grip mechanism on the other, giving you the option of wearing ordinary or special shoes. I have these fitted on a racing bike I use for long rides as well as popping to the shop, and they're brilliant.

There are two main types of shoes with cleats. Those marketed as mountain bike shoes are generally a little bulkier, but easier to walk in than the lighter, more plasticky 'road' type. You need to decide whether it is more important for you to be able to wander around with the shoes on, or to be as light and efficient as possible.

STYLE DIRECTORY

ALWAYS RIDING

Online emporium selling great range of high performing yet fashionable bike wear for both sexes: **www.alwaysriding.co.uk**

ANA NICHOOLA

London womenswear designer and cycling nut Anna Glowinski makes T-shirts out of bike-friendly bamboo as well as lovely jackets, and is developing bonkers but brilliant high heeled SPDs (clip-in cycling shoes): **www.ananichoola.co.uk**

BIONICON

Sporty but stylish bike wear for men and women. They make lovely softshell jackets and toasty merino wool tops: **www.bionicon.com**

BSPOKE (TFL)

Transport for London's okayish bike clothing line: **http://shop.tfl.gov.uk/Clothing-and-accessories/bspoke-cycling-clothing-collection.html**

BSPOKE TAILOR

Designer making custom cycling suits: **http://bspoketailor.blogspot.com**

CHARGE

British company specializing in fixed gear bicycles which also sells fashionable bike-friendly clothing under the brand Surface: **www.chargebikes.com**

CORDAROUNDS

US brand which sells the Bike To Work Pants. Ships worldwide: **www.cordarounds.com**

CYCLE CHIC

Online boutique selling beautiful bags, panniers, capes and clothes, as well as Dutch bikes: **www.cyclechic.co.uk**

CYCLODELIC

London-based designer Amy Fleuriot makes bags, panniers and clothes for fashion-conscious twentysomething female cyclists: **www.cyclodelic.co.uk**

DASHING TWEEDS

British textiles company making capes and suits for the two-wheeled sartorialist: **www.dashingtweeds.co.uk**

DO YOU VELO?

French online boutique selling stylish cycling trench coats. NB: the site was only in French at the time of writing: **www.doyouvelo.com**

HOWIES

UK brand with shops in London, Bristol and Cardigan as well as an online boutique which ships worldwide. Sells good-looking cycle-friendly gear for men and women, including lovely merino wool base layers and great trousers and jackets. Does a roaring trade in Love Me, Love My Bike T-shirts too: **www.howies.co.uk**

IBEX

US outdoor clothing company that sells dresses, hoodies, base layers, shorts and trousers for both sexes. Stocked in shops and online stores around the world:
www.ibexwear.com

KNOG

Fun Australian brand famed for its 'frog' bike lights. Also make cool gloves, hats and other accessories:
www.knog.com.au

MINX GIRL

UK-based website specializing in attractive cycle wear for women, with a bent towards mountain bikers:
www.minx-girl.com

NAU

Good-looking, eco-conscious US brand selling simple but classy outdoor clothing. Not specifically for cyclists, but very cycle-friendly:
www.nau.com

OSLOH

New York-based firm specializing in cool looking urban cycle gear, including jeans:
www.osloh.com

QUOC PHAM

Lovely leather bike shoes:
www.quocpham.com

RAPHA

Men's cycle gear lusted after by style-conscious cyclists the world over:
www.rapha.cc

SOMBRIO

Canadian company specializing in youth-oriented mountain bike wear. Makes particularly nice technical tops which look deceptively normal:
www.sombriocartel.com

SUGOI

American manufacturers of non-boring, performance sportswear for cyclists and triathletes. Also produces the Human Operated Vehicle (HOV) range, which taps into the bike-wear-disguised-as-ordinary-clothes market with biker jackets and more:
www.sugoi.com

SWOBO

US brand which specializes in nice-looking, ethical, technical bike gear in natural fabrics for both sexes:
www.swobo.com

SWRVE

US brand famed for its hardwearing but stylish cycling gear for men and women. The cycling knickers (three-quarter-length pants) come highly recommended:
www.swrve.co.uk

TOKYO FIXED GEAR

Trendy online emporium favoured by the fixie crowd; retails in pounds not yen, despite the name. Also has a real-life shop in Soho, central London:
www.tokyofixedgear.com

TWIN SIX

'Alternative cycling apparel' for men and ladies alike is the speciality of this US brand, stocked worldwide:
www.twinsix.com

URBAN HUNTER

Cool online shop selling T-shirts, jerseys, shorts, bags and caps – mostly for men:
www.urbanhunter.biz

WIGGLE

Huge online sports store that sells technical gear in the Tour de France mould, often heavily discounted:
www.wiggle.co.uk

LOOKING AFTER YOUR BIKE

here is no shame in not really understanding how your bike works, nor in wheeling
t to the nearest bike shop as soon as something goes wrong. Most people wouldn't
ry to fix their car when it packs in, so why their bike? It's supremely tedious when
cyclists get all high and mighty about maintenance, implying that anyone who doesn't
know how to adjust a derailleur or 'true' a wheel is an inferior being.

That said, it can't hurt to know the basics. It is good at least to be able to recognize
that something is wrong, even if you can't quite figure out what. And not knowing how
to take your tyre off and replace the inner tube when you get a puncture, for example,
s a real handicap unless you always cycle within walking distance of a bike mechanic.
Wouldn't you like to be able to pedal off into the countryside for a picnic, confident
that if you get a flat tyre you won't have to call for a minibus-sized taxi to pick you up?

Knowing how to perform other minor tweaks will also both save you money and make
cycling more enjoyable – whether it's silencing squeaky brakes, finding out what's
making that awful clicking noise, pumping your tyres up properly or simply knowing
which bits of your steed need oiling. This chapter will help you with all of this.

f you want to know more, buy a bike maintenance book. Recommended manuals
nclude The Bike Book by Fred Milson, Bicycle Repair Step-by-Step by Rob Van Der
Plas and Richard's Bike Book by Richard Ballantine. All are dated-looking tomes
featuring photographs of the ageing and bearded authors wearing criminal sweaters
and jeans pulled up to their nipples, but don't let that put you off. They tell you
everything you need to know, and can often be picked up very cheaply secondhand.

Better still, enrol on a bike maintenance course or get a knowledgeable friend to
show you the basics. It is very empowering being able to diagnose and cure your
bike's ills all by yourself. NB: if you choose the friend option, don't confuse 'show you
the basics' with 'fix it for you', otherwise you'll never learn.

When fiddling by yourself, try not to unscrew too many things at once. If you take bits
off, make sure you know where they came from and how to put them back on. I tend
to line things up in the order they came off.

There are many useful videos on the internet showing you how to care for your bike.
Some of the best are here: http://www.youtube.com/group/bicyclemaintenance

ANATOMY OF A BIKE

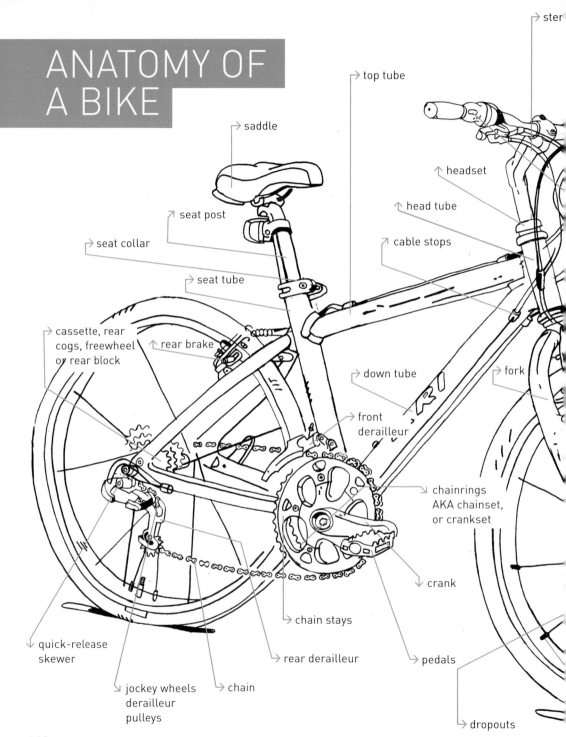

→ ster

→ top tube

→ saddle

↑ headset

→ seat post

← head tube

→ seat collar

↗ cable stops

→ seat tube

→ cassette, rear cogs, freewheel or rear block

↑ rear brake

→ down tube

→ fork

→ front derailleur

↳ chainrings AKA chainset, or crankset

↓ crank

↓ chain stays

↓ quick-release skewer

↘ rear derailleur

↘ pedals

↓ jockey wheels derailleur pulleys

↘ chain

↘ dropouts

→ handlebars

↘ brake levers

→ gears (frequently 24)

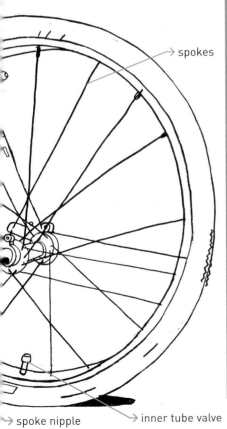

→ spokes

→ spoke nipple   → inner tube valve

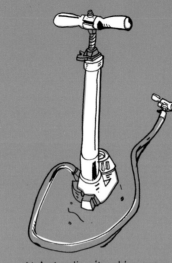

↘ A standing 'track' pump

↘ a set of tyre levers

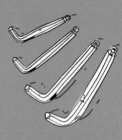

↘ a set of Allen keys
(either separate
or on a 'multi-tool'
device)

↘ an adjustable spanner

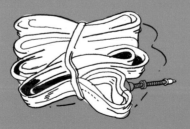

↘ a spare inner tube

OTHER ITEMS
↘ a puncture
repair kit

↘ cleaning rags

↘ a flat head and
a Phillips head
screwdriver

↘ bike-specific
lubricant

QUICK BIKE CHECK

1. ⬎ Check the tyres are pumped up properly and look for wear on the tread or for any cracks in the tyre. Worn tyres puncture easily.

2. ⬎ Spin the wheels. If they are wobbling around, they may have a buckle and need truing (straightening). This is not a job for a novice, but a bike shop can do it pretty quickly and cheaply.

3. ⬎ Check the brakes are working by squeezing the brake levers and pushing the bike forwards and backwards. Have a look at your brake pads – can you still see the ridges, or are they worn down? Check the pads are not touching the wheel rims and that they hit the rims head on.

4. ⬎ Make sure your headset is secure. Stand in front of your bike and put the front wheel between your knees, then try to move the handlebars from side to side. If the bars move without the wheel following, your stem needs tightening: this can usually be done with an Allen key.

5. ⬎ Run through the gears and check they are properly adjusted.

6. ⬎ Inspect the frame for any cracks.

7. ⬎ Check the chain is clean and lubricated.

HOW TO PUMP TYRES UP PROPERLY

The number one maintenance mistake novice cyclists make is not pumping their tyres up to the correct pressure. Just like car tyres, different bike tyres have different required pressures. Some years ago, I was absolutely convinced I was getting fat, as my easy commute had mysteriously begun to feel like a marathon. I couldn't understand why my previously nippy machine had turned into a sluggish donkey. Turned out I had been rolling at half the pressure my tyres actually needed. My tyres didn't look flat but, to all intents and purposes, they were.

To get your tyres inflated properly, forget using a mini hand pump. These little devices are fine for carrying on your frame and pumping enough air into your tyres after an emergency, but to do a proper job you need a 'track' or standing pump fitted with a pressure gauge. All but the meanest of bike shops will be happy to let you use their track pump whether or not you buy anything from them.

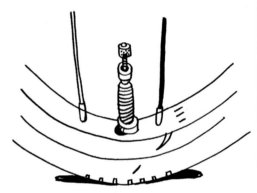

↘ Presta valve open

To talk of pumping tyres up is a bit of a misnomer. You are actually pumping up the inner tube which sits inside your tyre. These tubes are fitted with a valve to control the air pressure. There are two main kinds of valve. Prestas are smaller and more fiddly looking, and are common on road and hybrid bikes. You'll see the fatter Schrader valves most often on Dutch and mountain bikes.

If you are struggling with a pump, make sure it matches the kind of valve you have. Most bike pumps come with two different sized nozzles. The smaller is for Presta, the larger for Schrader. Track pumps tend to have a two-headed twin nozzle, and you just use the bit you need. Mini pumps usually have one reversible valve fitting, which you can unscrew and then rescrew on the other way around to fit the other kind of valve.

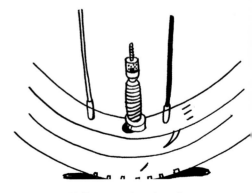

↘ Presta valve closed

PUMP IT

1. ↘ If your valve is covered with a dust cap, take it off.

2. ↘ If your inner tube has a Presta valve, undo the nut at the end of the valve as far as it can go (it won't come off unless you become violent). To check you've undone it enough, press the end down a little bit until you hear a hiss of escaping air. If the valve seems stuck, wiggle the stalk a little. If you have a Schrader valve, you don't need to unscrew anything.

3. ↘ Make sure you are using the right pump nozzle for your valve, then place the pump head square on to the valve. You'll hear a quick fizz of air rushing out of the valve; continue to press down. Don't worry. If there is a thumb-lock, put it on to stop everything moving around while you pump. If there is no closing mechanism, hold the head firmly on the valve as you pump.

4. ↘ Look on the side of the tyre for a series of numbers followed by the letters PSI. This tells you how much air you need to pump into your tyres. The skinnier your tyres, the harder they need to be. Generally, mountain bike tyres only need 30–40PSI, hybrids 50–85PSI and road bikes all the way up to 120PSI.

5. ↘ Pump air into the tyre by pulling the pump handle up and pushing down as if you are detonating a bomb. The pump should move easily. You should notice a difference in tyre firmness within seconds. If there are any problems and it's not working correctly, try reattaching the pump nozzle to the valve.

6. ↘ Inflate to the correct pressure, then carefully take off the pump nozzle. You'll hear another hiss. Don't panic – this happens to everyone.

7. ↘ If you have a Presta valve, screw the nut back on. Replace the dust cap.

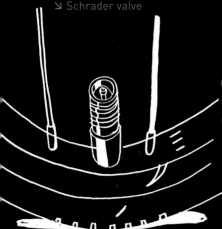

↘ Schrader valve

HOW TO CHANGE A FLAT TYRE

When cyclists whinge about getting a flat tyre, they actually mean that they have a flat inner tube. There may or may not be anything wrong with the actual tyre. The simplest way to fix a flat tyre is just to replace the inner tube, rather than faff around trying to mend it. If you only learn one aspect of bike maintenance, make it this one. Once you get the hang of it, it shouldn't take you more than twenty minutes (less if you're better at it than me), and you'll likely save yourself a tenner in bike shop fees. It can be a very frustrating experience at first, particularly when you're wrestling with a belligerent tyre that doesn't seem to want to go back on, but once you manage, you'll feel like the king of the world, I promise.

Modern tyres do not puncture often. Before tyre technology improved, punctures really were an everyday occurrence. In the 1908 London Olympics, the final of the 1,000 metres had to be abandoned when two of the top British riders, Charles Kingsbury and Victor Johnson, got flat tyres.

WHAT YOU NEED

- ⬈ A spare inner tube
- ⬈ A set of tyre levers
- ⬈ An adjustable spanner (only if you don't have quick release wheels)
- ⬈ A bike pump: a diddy one to carry with you for roadside repairs; a standing track pump to inflate tyres properly at home – or a canister of compressed gas
- ⬈ Latex gloves if you don't want to get your hands dirty

All this will fit in a small saddlebag or handbag with ease – apart from the track pump, of course.

TEN EASY STEPS

1 . **FULLY DEFLATE THE TYRE** _____
   ↘ If you haven't got a full-on flat, take the dust
   cap off the valve, and let the rest of the air out.

2 . **DISCONNECT THE BRAKES** _____
   ↘ You need to disconnect the brakes so that the
   tyre has more space to pass through. With quick
   release brakes, you pull up the cable by flipping
   an apostrophe-shaped lever.

3 . **TAKE THE WHEEL OFF** _____
   ↘ Turn your bike upside down. If you have a rear
   wheel puncture, change into the highest gear
   (smallest cog); this will make the wheel easier
   to get back on after-wards. On most modern
   bikes, you then need to undo the wheel's quick-
   release lever. Depending on who tightened
   it last, this can be quite stiff, so be prepared
   for a battle. Once you've loosened it, undo the
   thumbnut on the other side of the wheel and
   wangle the wheel free. Don't take the nut all the
   way off: they have a nasty habit of rolling down
   nearby drains. If it's the back wheel, you'll have
   to hold the chain out of the way by pulling at the
   derailleur with one hand while you take it off.
   This is invariably messy. If you don't have quick-
   release wheels, you'll have to unscrew a nut on
   each side using a spanner.

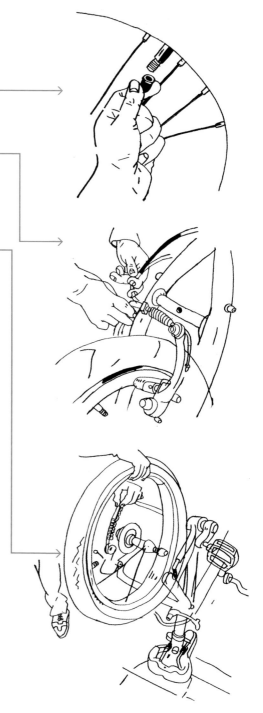

4. TAKE THE TYRE OFF

↘ You need the tyre levers for this bit, and the thinner your tyres, the harder this tends to be. Push the rounded end of the lever under the tyre and hook the other end on to a spoke.

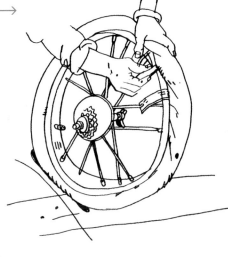

Wiggle the rounded end along a few inches so that it loosens that stretch of tyre. Do the same with the other levers, then go right round the tyre until one side is completely freed from the wheel and you can get at the inner tube. It's up to you whether you then take the whole tyre off or leave it half on. I prefer to remove the whole shebang, as it's easier to check for stones, etc. Then take off the punctured inner tube and either bin it or put it aside to mend later.

5. FIND THE BLIGHTER

↘ Run your fingers carefully along the inside and outside of the tyre to see if you can find what caused the puncture – a shard of glass, a drawing pin or a sharp stone are all common culprits. Failure to find the cause can result in the unspeakably exasperating experience of the tyre puncturing as soon as you set off again. If you've been really unlucky, the actual tyre might have been damaged and you'll have to patch it as best you can with gaffer tape – or a plaster or patch or whatever you can-find   and then mentally prepare yourself to buy a new tyre as soon as possible. Often, pumping up the inner tube when the tyre is still on will show you where the puncture happened, so you then know where on the tyre to check.

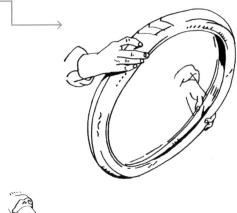

6. PUT THE NEW INNER TUBE ON

↘ First, ever so slightly inflate the tube to give it shape and so that it does not get pinched between the tyre lever and the rim. Then attach it to the wheel by putting the valve through the hole in the rim, and tuck the tube into the deepest part of the rim. Make sure the tube sits evenly and is not twisted. Don't screw on the rim nut yet.

7. PUT THE TYRE BACK ON

↘ This is the bit that occasionally reduces me to tears, as some tyres seem to go out of their way to not want to be put back where they belong. But persevere, and remember that if the tyre fitted before the puncture, it will again. Don't be tempted to use your tyre levers for this, or indeed any other tool, as you could accidentally puncture the new inner tube. Your fingers are all the tools you need.

Essentially, you carefully put the tyre back over the rim, starting at the valve. Pop it back in on both sides until it is in its place over the whole circumference of the wheel. Do one side completely first; it makes life a lot easier. Towards the end, it will likely get tough, and you might need to swear a little bit. I find it helps to smooth the entire tyre and tube down towards the valve to get more slack. Just when you think it will never ever go back in – Ta-da! It's on. Thank goodness for that.

8. PUT THE WHEEL BACK ON

↘ Check the tube is sitting evenly, then inflate it a little more and check it has straightened out inside the tyre. Screw the rim nut back on, make sure the brakes are still open, then slide the wheel over the fork ends, centre it as best you can and tighten the quick-release lever and thumbnut at the same time, using both hands, or rescrew the bolts. It's important to screw them on as tightly as you can, while still being confident you'll be able to undo them again – I once saw a man catapulted through the air as his front wheel came loose.

9. FULLY REINFLATE THE TYRE

↘ On the go, use a hand pump to get the tyre as hard as possible. As soon as you're near a track pump, inflate to the proper pressure.

10. RECONNECT THE BRAKES

↘ And you're off!

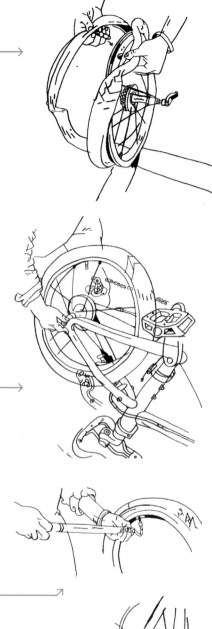

HOW TO MEND A PUNCTURE

If – for reasons of economy, ecology or necessity – you want to actually mend the puncture, here is how you do it. Attempting a roadside repair is a nightmare. Wherever possible, do this in the comfort of your own home. The jury is out on whether you should get self-adhesive patches or ones which require gluing, though everyone seems to agree that the self-adhesive ones lose their stickiness if they hang around unused for long.

1. LOCATE THE HOLE
↘ If it's a biggie, you'll be able to see it. Often, though, the cause of your puncture will be a sneaky little hole invisible to the naked eye. The easiest way to identify it is to pump a little air back into the tube and then put it under water. When you see bubbles, you have found the hole. If you have no water nearby, you'll need to use your ears and listen for air escaping. If you are somewhere too noisy, hold the tube really close to your face and see if you can feel air coming out.

2. MARK IT
↘ I find the pencils you get in puncture repair kits almost useless, especially if the tube is wet. Better is a bit of chalk, though you should use whatever you can find at the time – lipstick and eye pencil both work in an emergency.

3. ROUGH IT UP
↘ Using the bit of sandpaper you get in the kit, rough up the offending area and then wipe it clean.

4. PATCH IT
↘ When the tyre is clean and dry, apply the patch as per the instructions in the repair kit. Don't go mad with the glue, and make sure you leave it for five minutes or so until it is almost dry before sticking the patch on. Use the end of a tyre lever to press down on the patch as hard as you can and hold until it is securely glued in place. Once you're sure it's stuck fast, bend the patch in half and carefully remove the transparent covering.

An exhaustive guide to diagnosing and fixing punctures can be found on the old-school but wonderfully useful website belonging to the late bicycling enthusiast, Sheldon Brown: http://www.sheldonbrown.com/flats.html

SOD'S LAWS OF PUNCTURING

⬋ If you are going to get a puncture, it will be at the most inconvenient time, when you are late for a date, work or an important meeting, and have neglected to bring the necessary tools.

⬋ You will get more punctures on your rear tyre than the front, as the rear carries more weight. And it is fiddlier and messier to remove the rear wheel than the front one.

⬋ You will get more punctures in the rain, as more debris is washed on to the roads, and wet tyres are more susceptible to damage.

⬋ If you go around boasting about never getting a puncture, you soon will.

HOW TO AVOID PUNCTURES

⬋ Keep your tyres pumped up to the correct pressure. The optimal pressure (PSI) is marked on the side of the tyre. To reach this, you need a track pump with a pressure gauge.

⬋ Buy puncture resistant tyres. Look for anything marked Kevlar, which is the material bulletproof vests are made from. Many people swear by Schwalbe Marathon Plus or a Specialized Armadillo tyre. These are slightly less slick than serious roadie tyres, but you won't notice the difference unless you're cycling for sport and speed is of the essence. You could always put one only on the rear, which is far more likely to puncture.

⬋ Regularly check your tyres for wear and tear. If you have a spate of punctures on the same tyre, it's probably time to buy a new one. They're not that expensive.

⬋ Be vigilant when cycling past pubs and bars, where there is likely to be glass on the road.

⬋ In the rain, stay well clear of the gutter and drains, where debris is most likely to end up.

⬋ If you have a mountain bike, you could investigate tubeless tyres. You'll need tubeless specific rims for these, though, or you will have to convert those you ordinarily have using special gunge.

Tubeless tyres

Mountain bikers sometimes use tubeless tyres (also called USTs), which, as the name suggests, do not use inner tubes at all. You can only use these on tubeless/ UST specific rims, though some ordinary rims can be converted. Tubeless tyres are usually used in tandem with special tyre sealants, which improve the seal and are applied inside the tyre when installing on to the rim.

Tubular tyres

Serious road riders use these special tyres, which are glued on to the rims using tape or cement. Tubulars are lighter than conventional tyres and provide a smoother ride, but are far more expensive and are much harder to repair once punctured.

CO_2 cartridges

These little canisters of carbon dioxide are useful if you are racing and can't waste time pumping up a tyre after a puncture. Used with an adapter, they blow tyres up in seconds. But they only work once, so don't mess it

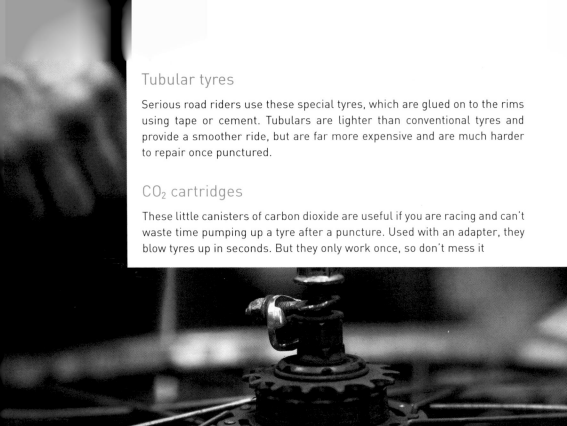

WASH 'N' GO

The biggest favour you can do your bike is not to let it get too dirty and to keep it well oiled. This isn't so much a matter of pride as of mechanics – gunk-covered bikes ride badly and their components wear out quickly. A proper cleaning and lubricating routine is a bit of a rigmarole, especially if, like me, you live in a flat with no garden and don't have a special stand to clamp the bike into. But, on those occasions I set aside an hour to do it properly, I often find myself in a weird, Zen-like state, finding peculiar satisfaction in scrubbing my derailleur with a toothbrush and polishing every spoke, something the teenagers on my estate seem to find endlessly amusing.

If you ride every day, other books suggest you wash and oil your bike once a week. This is a lovely theory, but unless you have encountered dreadful weather or taken short cuts across muddy fields, it is probably unnecessary. Rare is the day I don't use my bike, and I only give it a proper clean every couple of months or before a major expedition.

Don't be tempted to go to your local garage and use a high pressure hose to clean your bike. It is too strong, and water could get into internal components. But a gentle garden hose is fine.

WHAT YOU NEED

- ⩒ A bucket of hot, soapy water. Washing-up liquid is OK
- ⩒ A special degreasing agent such as Muck-Off, to be sprayed directly on to the really grubby bits
- ⩒ A sponge or soft rag
- ⩒ An old toothbrush or, if you prefer, a set of proper bike-cleaning brushes
- ⩒ Bike-specific lubricant. You are supposed to use different oils for different bits of your bike – liquid for the chain, brake cables and bolts; grease for overhauling bearings and threads (an unlikely task for an amateur). Being a bit of a slattern, I just use a lightish all-round liquid oil such as Finish Line Cross Country for everything. Many people consider household oils such as WD-40 to be a bicycle's nemesis, swearing they can ruin a chain by actually stripping away any existing lubricant. But I've used them in emergencies to no obvious ill effect

⌐ A chain-cleaning machine is very useful but not necessary, as you can
a toothbrush

⌐ In an ideal world, you'll have a frame stand to clamp your bike into, This will make
it easy to turn the pedals and reach inaccessible parts, but you can manage without

You'll probably feel a bit of a saddo watching it, but there is a very good video
called 'washing and lubing your bike' on this site: http://www.youtube.com/
group/bicyclemaintenance

THE WASH

1. ⌐ Spray bike wash fluid all over your bike and leave for a minute or so
to let the degreasing agents do their thing. Pay special attention to the
chainset, front and rear mechs and chain, as they will be the oiliest and
dirtiest bits.

2. ⌐ Use a brush to poke around your bike to dislodge any bits and bobs stuck
behind hard-to-reach parts, and spray more fluid there if necessary.

3. ⌐ Starting at the top of your bike, so that you don't dirty already-clean
bits, dip the sponge or rag into the soapy water to wipe down the frame,
saddle, handlebar and stem, and seat post.

4. ⌐ Now is the time to tackle the chain and gear system. If you have a
chain-cleaning machine, follow the instructions to clamp the device to
the chain and slowly turn the pedals so that all of the chain goes through
the machine's internal brushes. Otherwise, dip the toothbrush in more
degreaser and then scrub each link of the chain. Use a sponge to clean
between the teeth of the sprockets on your rear wheel cassette and the
front and rear derailleur.

5. ⌐ Take the wheels out and sponge down the inside of the frame forks
and underneath the brake callipers and pads. Then clean the wheel rims
thoroughly. Squeaky brakes are often caused by dirt, so don't scrimp on
this part.

If I'm being lazy and the weather is bad outside, I sometimes give my bike a quick
once-over in my hallway when my neighbours have gone to bed, using baby wipes.
Seems to do the trick.

THE LUBE

Before you start oiling, make sure the bike is dry, then lubricate the chain, holding a cloth under it as you sparingly apply oil to each link, slowly turning the pedals as you go. Work through all of your gears to get oil on each sprocket and cog. If oil drips off, you've gone overboard, and need to wipe most of it away. The chain should feel dry, with just a smidgen of oil covering it.

Less frequently, you need to give a tiny squirt to:

↘ All brake cables, where they go in or out of the cable casings
↘ The front and rear hubs (including the freewheel)
↘ The front and rear mech
↘ Pedal axles and any moving parts on your cleats
↘ Any bolts

NB: Never oil your brake blocks or wheel rims. It will stop them working.

KEEPING YOUR BIKE SCHTUM

A healthy bike is a silent bike. When yours starts making horrible noises – squealing, screeching, clicking, crunching – diagnose the problem and get it sorted before it sends you batty.

There is an excellent and comprehensive guide to keeping your bike quiet on this website: http://www.jimlangley.net/wrench/keepitquiet.html

But here are the common causes:

SQUEAKY BRAKES

Screeching brakes are not dangerous, but they are irritating in the extreme. The first thing to do is ensure your wheel rims are clean, as well as your brake pads. Dust or grime is very often the problem. If that doesn't sort it out, you could fiddle with the position of your brake pads to make sure they hit the rims square on. They shouldn't be touching the tyres at all. Most brake pads feature a mechanism for making this adjustment. It can be done in a minute or so by someone who knows what they are doing, so be nice to a bike mechanic and they might do it for free, or follow the instructions for your particular sort of brakes in a bicycle maintenance book. Sometimes, though, brakes just won't shut up, however much you clean and readjust them. I couldn't silence mine until I replaced both front and back brake pads.

CLICKY GEARS

You may have badly adjusted gears, or are riding in an ill-advised gear, which puts the chain at an extreme angle (e.g. being on the small chainring and the smallest cog). Avoid. If your gears appear to be slipping, i.e. not changing smoothly, the chain might be gunked up. Clean and lubricate it thoroughly. If that doesn't work, you'll either need to learn more about gears from a bike maintenance book, or take it to your local bike shop. If the sprockets on the back of your bike no longer have vicious, evenly pointy teeth but have started to look a little more mellow, prepare to replace worn-out chains and cassettes/freewheels, which isn't cheap.

SQUEALING CHAIN

It needs oiling. If you look at the chain and see bright, shiny links, you've waited too long to add lube. Always try to keep a thin film of lube on the chain, and you'll prevent rust, squeaks, crunchy gear changing and premature wear. Changing your chain occasionally (say every 1,000 miles) is the best thing you can do for your bike. It is a cheap part to replace, but if you let a chain get too worn or rusty, you will have to change the cassette (the sprockets/cogs on the back wheel) at the same time, which is much more expensive.

CREAKY PEDALS

Make sure the crank arm is well lubricated and that you've got the pedals on tight enough. Cleats ('clipless pedals', see p. 66) can also cause problems. If your cleats are metal, grease them lightly, and remember not to wear them in the house afterwards.

NOISY WHEELS

First, check nothing is caught in the spokes. Sometimes, reflectors slightly catch on a spoke, so manoeuvre them about a bit and make sure they're on tightly. Sometimes, the spokes themselves are to blame, especially when they are old. To shut them up, apply a drop of oil at each spoke intersection. Then go around and squeeze pairs of spokes with your hands, which will let the oil work between the spokes. Remember to wipe off any excess oil once you're done. Noisy wheels can also be caused by loose bearings in the wheel hubs, but don't start taking the hub apart unless you know what you're doing.

EMERGENCY REPAIRS

If your bike breaks in the middle of nowhere, there are various field repairs you can carry out to get you to the nearest station. Though it sounds a bit Famous Five, you can stuff a flat tyre with grass and/or newspaper in an emergency, and you can just about fix a broken chain with a paper clip. Just ride gingerly home.

GETTING YOUR BIKE SERVICED

Unless you are an accomplished amateur bike mechanic, you'll need to get your bike professionally serviced at least once a year, ideally twice if you ride every day – once in spring, to prepare for a summer in the saddle, and once in autumn, to get ready for the winter. If you just need a quick fix – a puncture mended or brakes tweaked – many shops offer a drop-in service at the start of the day.

Most bike shops offer different levels of service, from a basic gears-'n'-brakes plus lube job right the way up to the Full Monty, which involves the bike being stripped down, with each cable and bearing checked and regreased and replaced if necessary. Some people baulk at the price of a proper service, which often costs £100 or more. But think of it as your insurance against future problems. A well looked after bike can last decades; a poorly maintained machine won't last a year. You wouldn't expect a car to pass its MOT if it had never been serviced; the same is true of bicycles.

Before you take your bike in for a service, give it a good wash. It will encourage the mechanic to spend time fixing your bike rather than getting it clean enough to see what he or she is doing.

Tales of servicing rip-offs are common so, if you can, only use a reputable bike shop that has been recommended to you by friends. Ideally, get someone who knows about bikes to diagnose the problem before you get there so that no one can con you into replacing irrelevant bits of your bike. Bad bike shops make money by carrying out unnecessary repairs – taking off perfectly fine brake blocks or cables and charging you for new ones is the classic tactic, or announcing that you need to buy new tyres.

TIPS

1. ↘ Agree a price and completion date in advance, and make the bike shop promise to check with you before embarking on any additional work.

2. ↘ Remember that you will have to pay extra for any new parts.

3. ↘ Before you leave the shop, check everything seems in order. Failure to re-attach brakes is a classic.

4. ↘ Unless you had a bad experience there, take your bike to be serviced at the place which sold it to you. Especially if the bike is still quite new, the shop might be obliged (or feel obliged) to fix the problem for free.

BIKE MAINTENANCE FAQS

Q. WHY HAS MY BIKE BECOME MORE DIFFICULT TO RIDE?

↘ You probably need to pump your tyres up. It's amazing what a difference it makes – you'll feel like you're riding a different bike when you've inflated them properly. Use a track pump with a pressure gauge rather than a hand pump to get tyres to the right pressure (look for the PSI number on the wheel to see what pressure your tyres should be at). If you have a road bike or hybrid, your thumb shouldn't make a dent if you push the side of the tyre. Chunkier tyres require less pressure.

Q. WHAT DO I DO IF THE CHAIN COMES OFF?

↘ Put it back on. Sometimes you can keep your hands clean by simply changing up a gear. Pedal lightly and finesse the chain back into place. If this doesn't work, you'll have to physically put it back on by lifting it up and on to a cog. This is a messy job, so wear latex gloves if you have a pair handy in your saddlebag. If the chain has slipped off one of the chain rings in front, push the rear derailleur forward a touch while you use your other hand to put the chain back on a chain ring. If the chain has slipped off the sprockets on the rear, try to put it back on. If you can't, you'll have to take the wheel off.

Q. HOW CAN I GET THIS OIL OFF MY HANDS?

↘ Use washing-up liquid and sugar. Only add water when you've worked it all over your hands. Or you could use a special detergent such as Swarfega.

Q. HOW CAN I GET OIL OFF MY CLOTHES?

↘ Oil stains are easier to banish than red wine, as long as you don't put the stained garment through an ordinary wash before treating it. Often an ordinary stain remover will do the trick, but you can also use bike degreasing fluid, oven cleaner, washing-up liquid or shampoo, depending on the fragility of the garment. If the oil has dried, some people swear by sprinkling some baby powder on it, letting it set, shaking it off and washing as normal.

Q. WHY DO I ALWAYS END UP WITH OIL ON MY LEG?

↘ Because it keeps touching the grubby rear mechanism, I imagine. Try to train yourself to put your left foot on the floor when you stop at traffic lights or wherever, as that side doesn't have any oily bits.

Q. WHY DO I KEEP GETTING PUNCTURES?

↘ You may just be unlucky. But chances are, you probably need a new tyre – either your old one is worn out, has sustained a bad tear or there is something sharp sticking out of your wheel rim. To see if that's the case, take off the tyre and run your finger carefully along the metal rim of the wheel. Sometimes spokes poke out of the rim tape, and then you'll have to either file down the spoke (tricky) or replace the rim tape (easier).

Q. I KEEP GETTING PUNCTURES BUT THERE DOESN'T SEEM TO BE A HOLE IN MY INNER TUBE

↘ Your valve might be leaking. You can check if this is the case without removing the inner tube by filling an eggcup with water and dipping the valve in. If there is a stream of bubbles, you have a leak. Unlucky. If you have a Presta valve, you'll have to replace the whole tube. If it's a Schrader, you can just screw in a new insert, but most people opt to replace the inner tube too.

Q. WHY DO I KEEP BENDING/BREAKING THE VALVE ON MY INNER TUBE WHEN PUMPING THE TYRE UP?

↘ This used to happen to me all the time when I was a bit cavalier with my hand pump. It never happens if you use a track pump and, when pumping, do your best to support the valve so that, when you're inflating the tyre, the valve is not taking the brunt of your pumping force. If you do break the valve, you have to replace the whole inner tube, I'm afraid, as sooner or later it will fail.

Q. WHY IS MY SADDLE SO UNCOMFORTABLE?

↘ It might be a rubbish saddle, or simply the wrong one for you – women's bikes often come with men's saddles for reasons I've yet to fathom. But you may also need to adjust it. Try tipping it a few degrees up or down and see if that helps.

CYCLING SAFELY

The fear of getting knocked off is one of the biggest deterrents to cycling. It is a perfectly rational concern – cars, lorries and buses are, after all, heavy great lumps of metal capable of wiping out a vulnerable little bicycle with one ill-considered swerve. But contrary to popular belief, you do not need a death wish to get on your bike. In fact, Department for Transport figures from 2007 showed that, statistically, cycling is safer than walking per mile travelled. Remember, too, that because of the health benefits associated with cycling, using a bike regularly is far more likely to prolong your life than cut it short. One Danish study published in the Archives of Internal Medicine in the year 2000 monitored more than 30,000 people over 14.5 years and found that those who did not cycle to work experienced a 39 per cent higher mortality rate than those who did.

More good news: cycling gets safer as more people do it. For instance, a 91 per cent increase in cycle use on London's main roads between 2001 and 2008 was accompanied by a 33 per cent reduction in the number of cyclist casualties over roughly the same period, according to the Safety In Numbers campaign by the CTC, the national cyclists' organization. The same trend has been witnessed in many other places around the world – in the Netherlands, the level of bicycle traffic increased by 30 per cent between 1980 and 1990, yet annual cyclist deaths fell by one third.

Cycling is also far safer than many other physical activities. Figures from 1986 showed that you were forty-one times more likely to die fishing than cycling. Only golf and rambling were safer, according to the study. Relative to cycling (index 1), the fatality index for tennis was 4.2, football 4.9, swimming 7, horseriding 29, climbing 137 and 'airsports' 450.

In twenty years of regular cycling, five in the traffic-choked streets of London, I have never been knocked off. I do worry a little that by declaring this I'll be crushed by a juggernaut and this book will be published posthumously, but I hope it gives you some reassurance regardless.

Whether or not you are convinced, there are a number of things you can do – or, more importantly, not do – to drastically increase your chances of staying in one piece when out on your bike.

THE THREE GOLDEN RULES

1 . SHUN THE KERB

The best advice I can give you is to behave like a car: you have just as much of a right to take up space as any other vehicle. Remember the slogan of the international cycling movement Critical Mass: 'We are traffic.' Refuse to be pushed into the gutter. Travel towards the middle of any lane you're in. This takes guts at first. Often people are more worried about getting beeped than staying safe and so hug the kerb apologetically to let drivers pass without them having to change lanes. This is a bad idea. So you get honked at? At least the honker has seen you. You may worry they will run into the back of you, but they won't. Instead, they will be forced to slow down and will only overtake when the coast is clear.

You are infinitely better off in the middle of the lane than cosying up to the kerb, where vehicles will squeeze past you at scary proximity, often not even noticing you until their wing mirror hits your handlebars – or worse. Being too far left when turning at a junction is also problematic, because it encourages cars to sidle up alongside you and make the turn first – potentially, straight into your path. There's another reason you don't want to hang out by the kerb: it's where all the puncture-causing detritus ends up.

2. LOOK BACK

To stay safe on a bike, you need to learn how to look behind you while going forwards. Car drivers are taught to look in their mirrors every few seconds – good cyclists keep glancing back almost as often. Knowledge is power: if you can see who is behind you, you won't be surprised if they do something silly. And by looking over your shoulder, ideally right into the eyes of the driver behind, you also significantly reduce the chances of them attempting any ill-advised manoeuvring. Looking at someone lets them know that you know they are there. It also suggests that you are about to make a move. Car drivers are taught the 'mirror/signal/manoeuvre' mantra. Cyclists should do the same, but substituting the mirror bit for a head swivel.

3. CYCLE LIKE YOU MEAN IT

Be confident. In his safe cycling guide *Cyclecraft*, John Franklin says 'the biggest mistake cyclists make is being too submissive when sharing the roads, somehow feeling that they must always allow priority to motor vehicles.' Confidence also means executing manoeuvres with aplomb. Don't half-arse your arm signals; don't waver when changing lanes or turning right. Losing your bottle midway through doing something is often far more dangerous than ploughing on ahead with it.

SAFETY ACCESSORIES

MUST I DON A LUMINOUS TABARD/CAGOULE?

No, particularly not in the daytime. I don't. I took this decision not just out of vanity, but mostly because I believe it is far more important to cycle in a visible position on the road than to swathe myself in fluorescent fabrics. By all means wear the Day-glo gear if it makes you feel safer, but all the luminosity in the world is no use if you're cycling up the back end of a truck, out of sight of the driver's mirrors. At night, wearing anything reflective is a very good idea – the new generation of cycling gear that doesn't look like cycling gear often has discreet reflective cuffs, weaves and hems which look normal by day but glimmer by night (see chapter 3). You could also slip on a reflective sash or clip, or something like a Claq, made by TWOnFRO (www. twonfro.com). It's a strip of reflective malleable plastic with a magnet at each end which you fix to a piece of clothing, hair or bike.

SHOULD I GET INDICATORS?

Though you can buy clip-on bike indicators, they are no substitute for sticking your arm out and signalling your intentions. Car drivers know to look out for arm signals; if they notice your flashing indicators, they may well not understand what they mean.

WHAT ABOUT A FLAG?

If you feel a flag will help drivers see you, go ahead, but be aware that they look ridiculous on any bike not transporting a primary-school-aged child.

DO I NEED LIGHTS?

Yes. Cycling without lights is illegal and stupid. As well as having a white light on the front and a red on the rear, bikes are legally supposed to be fitted with a red rear reflector and, if manufactured after 1 October 1985, amber pedal reflectors. Note that it is no longer illegal to ride with flashing lights, though the Highway Code recommends that cyclists who are riding in areas without street lighting use a steady front lamp.

THE ENEMIES OF CYCLING

1. CAR DOORS

Getting 'doored' is one of the biggest risks cyclists face when travelling in urban areas. In 2003, more cyclists in London were seriously injured when hitting an open door, or swerving to avoid a suddenly opening door, than as a result of any other conflict.

At the risk of stating the blindingly obvious, the only thing you can do to avoid this very painful occurrence is to always cycle at least a car door's width away from parked vehicles. Sometimes, particularly on narrow streets when cars are coming at you in the opposite direction, this can take a certain amount of courage. But stay firm. Cycle slowly, look/signal/smile at the oncoming driver, and 90 per cent of the time they will slow down or stop to let you past. If they don't – the sods – you'll be going at a sensible enough pace that you can pull in safely and give them your best disappointed look as they pass.

Don't assume only parked cars pose a danger. A friend of mine got doored weaving through stationary traffic when the passenger of one car decided to get out and walk.

2. LEFT-TURNING LORRIES

A great number of cyclist deaths are caused by the same, depressing – but avoidable – scenario: lorries turning left and not seeing cyclists who have come up on the inside.

It's a tempting manoeuvre. You're making your way through a queue of traffic, overtaking stationary vehicles on the inside lane ('undertaking'), and then you reach a great big truck. The truck is the only thing between you and the traffic lights, so you edge your way alongside it, figuring you'll be ahead and away by the time the lights change. Don't do it. Time it wrong and the lights will go green, the lorry will turn left and you'll be underneath it.

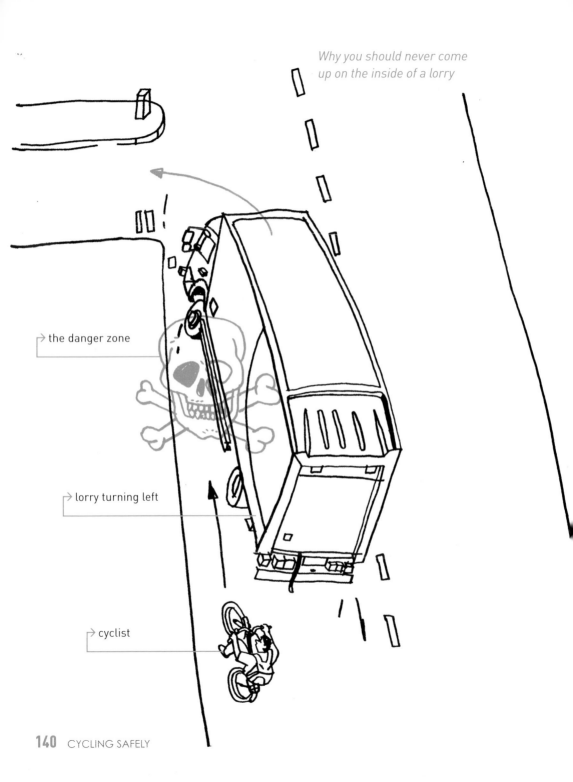

Why you should never come up on the inside of a lorry

the danger zone

lorry turning left

cyclist

Ever keen to beat motorized traffic, I used to do it quite a lot – until I met Paul Wood from the Metropolitan Police, who has been investigating traffic collisions in central London for the past fifteen years.

Many people imagine that lorries kill cyclists by speeding by and knocking them off with great force, but this isn't the case, according to Wood. He says:

Generally, the collision occurs at junctions where the lorry is perhaps going no more than 5mph. The cyclist is usually going quite a bit faster, say 10–12mph, and they often think they can undertake the slow lorry and get ahead.

What happens is that the cyclist comes up alongside the lorry on the left-hand side, often close enough to touch it, which generally means they are out of sight of the lorry's mirrors – especially on older vehicles, which aren't fitted with as many. In this position, they can't see the lorry's indicators either.

The lorry then goes to turn left, having not seen the cyclist, and generally just clips them, giving them a little nudge which is just enough to destabilize them and make them fall to the ground. The lorry driver won't even feel the hit, and almost certainly won't see it, so will continue turning, right over the fallen cyclist, who is then crushed underneath. The first thing the driver will often know about it is when they hear the crunching of metal underneath them, by which point it is all too late.

Never go up on the inside of lorries is my only real advice for cyclists. Everything else, to my mind – whether or not you wear a helmet or reflective gear, whether you run red lights, all that sort of thing – is trivial in comparison.

Remember, too, that articulated vehicles take a different path to cars, motorbikes and bicycles. While the cab takes a more or less normal path round corners, albeit in the middle of the road, the trailer follows a much tighter arc. Fail to anticipate this, and you run the risk of getting pulled under the truck or squashed against those awful fences lining many major roads (the ones which are supposed to make things safer by discouraging pedestrians from crossing, but which many traffic experts now believe to pose more dangers than benefits).

3. CYCLE LANES

Cycle lanes have popped up all over the country of late, particularly since the very welcome introduction of the national cycle network in 2000. These lanes are marked either by a solid white line – which indicates a mandatory lane that other vehicles aren't allowed to cross – or a broken white line which indicates an 'advisory' lane.

But don't assume, just because a bit of road has a nice picture of a bicycle painted on it, that you have to ride in it. Indeed, sometimes you'd be mad to. Though cycle lanes which are completely separate from ordinary roads are often a dream to navigate (these are actually called 'cycle tracks') the reality is that all too many bike lanes appear to be designed by traffic planners who have apparently a) never ridden a bike before, b) never driven a car on roads where there are cyclists before or c) have such a violent hatred of cyclists that they want to see us all so badly disabled we'll never get in the saddle again.

The most common problem with bike lanes is that they encourage cyclists to stick to the far left of roads, which causes the problems outlined above with left-turning vehicles, particularly HGVs.

The other issue occurs when cycle paths are divided from the main road by bollards or raised bits of kerb. Though good in theory, all too often they are punctuated with breaks to allow cars to turn right across them into side roads, frequently without warning. Be especially careful with these when going into major junctions and at roundabouts.

Sometimes cycle lanes simply aren't wide enough to be worth it – in one infamous case, the lane was so narrow that the white bicycle logo couldn't fit into it. Though the UK government recommends that bike lanes be at least 1.5m wide, there is no legal minimum width for a cycle lane. Still you can complain to your local council if they create something particularly idiotic. Some clever local authorities like to place random bollards in the middle of bike lanes too, or start them in places that are almost impossible for cyclists to access safely.

In 2009, a study by Leeds and Bolton universities showed that cyclists are in much more danger of being hit by cars on roads that include cycle lanes because they encourage motorists to drive closer when overtaking bicycles. The study said that on roads without cycle lanes, drivers 'consciously perform an overtaking manoeuvre'. On roads with cycle lanes, they treat the space between the centre line and the outside edge of the cycle lane as exclusively their territory and make less adjustment for cyclists, allegedy.

Lanes are also sometimes in stupid places. In 2006, a 25-year-old man was found guilty of 'inconsiderate cycling' when he stuck to a main road in Telford rather than crossing three lanes of busy traffic to ride on a segregated cycle track. Daniel Cadden was cycling fast downhill on a single-lane approach to a roundabout when he was stopped by police, who believed that the position he had taken in his lane was forcing cars to cross the solid white line in the centre of the road illegally in order to overtake. But rather than stop the cars that had broken the law, these knuckle-headed officers decided to charge Cadden with obstructing the highway. He was found guilty by a District Judge in Telford Magistrates Court and fined £100 with £200 costs, though the decision was overturned on appeal the following year.

The Highway Code was later changed to clarify the legal position on using cycle lanes, and now reads: 'Use cycle routes, advanced stop lines, cycle boxes and toucan crossings unless at the time it is unsafe to do so. Use of these facilities is not compulsory and will depend on your experience and skills, but they can make your journey safer.'

A famous study analysing Milton Keynes's 'redway' cycle paths showed that the cycle path network suppressed rather than encouraged cycling and proved to be consistently less safe than the town's unrestricted main roads.

Segregated cycle lanes can also have the negative effect of worsening the unpleasant apartheid which exists between bicycles and cars. Rather than encouraging the idea that cyclists form part of the ordinary traffic, with just as much right to space and respect as those using any other vehicle, they further the notion that bikes don't belong on the road proper and reinforce the lowly status of cyclists. That's why drivers sometimes give you a hard time for shunning a bike lane and travelling on the main road. Ignore them. Only use bike lanes if you are genuinely safer and happier doing so.

4. MANHOLE COVERS

Avoid, especially in the rain. They get awfully slippery. Beware, too, of drain covers delicately installed with their slots running in the direction of the road instead of at 90 degrees. Innocently ride over one of these, and you may well find yourself with your front wheel heading towards the sewers – and your body quite possibly going over your handlebars. Amazingly, these are not illegal, though most local councils and highway agencies have realized they're not just cretinous but could also open them up to all sorts of legal action.

5 . POTHOLES

In the UK, there is, on average, one pothole every 120 yards (110 metres), according to the made-up-sounding Asphalt Industry Alliance. I can well believe it as I dodge them on the same roads every day. In an ideal world, you'll spot a pothole before you hit it, but if it catches you unaware, stand up out of your seat and shift your weight to the back of the bike to cushion the blow. It is not always possible, but if you do have to dodge a pothole, try to give the traffic behind you a quick glance or signal to let them know what you're about to do.

Local councils are responsible for the upkeep of most of the roads cyclists are likely to use. While they generally have some mechanism for members of the public to report potholes, they tend to be rather better at taking reports than acting on them. In 2009, Navestock Parish Council in Essex had the cheek to claim the holes in the road helped slow down traffic, and said that they would therefore not be repairing them.

If you come off your bike because you hit a pothole, you may be able to claim compensation. In 2009, a cyclist injured in this very scenario was awarded £7,600 by his local council in West Berkshire, when his solicitor proved that they were in breach of their duties under Section 58 of the Highways Act 1980 – which states the highway must not be dangerous to traffic.

You can also report potholes on www.fillthathole.org.uk, which allows users to zoom into any road in the UK and mark the location of a crater. The clever website then automatically emails the local authority, which is then expected to take action. It takes no longer than two minutes to use, and if a problem is ignored and subsequently someone crashes, it is possible to prove that the council knew about it.

HOW TO . . .

. . . SIGNAL

To a certain breed of cyclist, using a hand to tell other road users where they are going – rather than simply to tell an errant driver where to go – is unthinkable.

In the vast majority of instances, this reluctance has nothing to do with an inability to lift one hand from the bars and everything to do with the flawed view that using an arm signal is about as necessary as learning Esperanto. For these signalling refuseniks, applying any of what they learned in cycling proficiency to real life is like actually drinking no more than the number of units the government recommends – an ideal, rather than a realistic proposition.

But sticking an arm out to signal is not for lily-livered, gutless conformists. It's a fine way of registering your intentions. Think how infuriating it is when a car doesn't indicate. Not signalling is exactly the same thing.

Three related matters:

1. ↘ Put your back into it. If you're going to signal, make it a good one. You are not at school trying to pretend you're too cool to put your hand up properly.

2. ↘ Don't just assume a quick little arm signal is enough to plough on with whatever manoeuvre you had in mind. Before you signal, turn around, check what's coming and, if possible, look in the eyes of the person behind. That way they will expect you to make a move.

3. ↘ Forget about the flappy arm-up-and-down signal you learned in cycling proficiency which apparently signals your intention to stop. People will think you're trying to take off.

. . . NEGOTIATE A MULTI-LANE ROUNDABOUT

The Highway Code is rubbish on roundabouts, with its first piece of advice being 'You may feel safer walking your cycle round on the pavement or verge.' Assuming, however, you want to give roundabouts a go, there are six main things you should do:

1. ↘ Choose the same lane you would if you were in a car, and position yourself in the middle of that lane. So if you're taking the first exit, stay in the left-hand lane; if you're going straight ahead, stay in the middle; if you're going right or all the way round, keep right.

2. ↘ Steer well clear of the outside edge of the roundabout when you're in the left

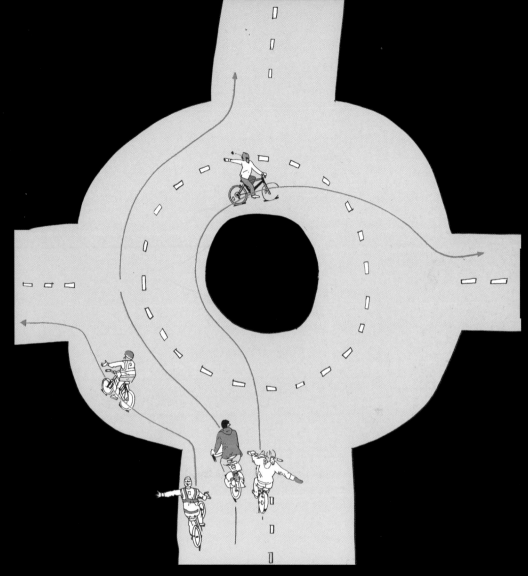

3. ↘ If you're going straight on or <u>right</u>, make sure you look behind you and signal when you are moving into the left-hand lane to make your exit.

4. ↘ Keep well clear of the give way markings as you pass the roundabout's entry points to give yourself the best chance of being seen by waiting motorists.

5. ↘ Watch out for vehicles crossing your pathto leave or join the roundabout.

6. ↘ As ever, try to make eye contact with any motorist relevant to your manoeuvre.

BIKE SAFETY FAQS

Q. CAN I CYCLE IN BUS LANES?

↘ Yes, unless there is a sign telling you specifically not to. Ignore irate bus drivers beeping or driving up your bottom as you slow them down approaching a bus stop. You have a right to be there, but don't pass between the kerb and a bus when it is at a stop, otherwise you'll knock people getting on or off. Be very careful when overtaking a bus or leaving a bus lane, as you will be entering a busier traffic flow. If you object to sharing a lane with buses – and often motorcycles – you don't have to. Car drivers sometimes try to push you into the bus lane, but ride firm and do whatever you feel is safest.

Q. ARE CARS ALLOWED TO IGNORE ADVANCED STOP LINES AT TRAFFIC LIGHTS?

↘ No. But they do, all the time, and never get done for it. Advance stop lines (ASLs) mark a segregated section of the road just in front of traffic lights where cyclists can supposedly wait in safety for the lights to change. The Highway Code states:

*Motorists, including motorcyclists, **MUST** stop at the first white line reached if the lights are amber or red and should avoid blocking the way or encroaching on the marked area at other times, e.g. if the junction ahead is blocked. If your vehicle has proceeded over the first white line at the time that the signal goes red, you MUST stop at the second white line, even if your vehicle is in the marked area. Allow cyclists time and space to move off when the green signal shows.*

As far as I've been able to ascertain, no motorist in the UK has ever been prosecuted for sitting in an ASL. If you can safely get to an ASL, good for you. It's nice not having to breathe in exhaust fumes. But be really careful trying to reach an ASL via a kerbside cycle lane in case the lights change before you reach it, and a vehicle turns left into your path. If you've entered the box from the left, it is very dangerous to turn right by cycling across the waiting area. And try to resist the temptation to creep out of the ASL when the lights are red to get a head-start on the cars behind you.

Q. WHEN SHOULD I RING MY BELL?

↘ I hate over-enthusiastic bell-ringing and, where possible, prefer to shout out a cheery 'Coming through!' or 'Excuse me, please!' I save my bell for cycling along towpaths. If I'm going round a blind corner or under a narrow bridge, two tings warns others I am on the approach.

OTHER GOLDEN RULES

- ⬎ If you can't see a vehicle's mirrors, the driver can't see you.
- ⬎ Only undertake with extreme caution.
- ⬎ Anticipate the worst. Never assume what other people are about to do.
- ⬎ Always make sure you have enough space to cope with unforeseen circumstances, such as the doors of parked cars springing open without warning, or the car in front stopping suddenly. You might not need to keep the proverbial two chevrons apart, but bikes need space to come to a stop too. In *Cyclecraft*, John Franklin recommends maintaining about 2 metres (nearly 7 feet) for every 5km/h or so, with an absolute minimum of 3 metres (10 feet).
- ⬎ Never tailgate at speed. Car brakes are better than bike brakes.
- ⬎ If you get into a difficult spot, pull over.
- ⬎ If you're on a shared use cycle path, remember that pedestrians have priority.

Ghost bikes

If you ever see a bike painted white and chained to railings or a lamp post, it is probably a ghost bike, left there in memory of a cyclist killed at that spot. The first ghost bikes were created in St Louis, Missouri in 2003, and they have since appeared in over ninety locations throughout the world. For more information, see www. ghostbikes.org

ACCIDENTS

If you are involved in an accident, first of all, check that you are OK. If you hurt yourself, especially if you hit your head, make sure you receive rapid medical attention, even if it means taking yourself to casualty. It's rare, but an apparently innocuous bump to the head can quickly develop into a life-threatening brain injury if it's not seen to.

If your accident was caused by a pothole or some other inexcusable road defect, you may be entitled to compensation. Once you've sorted yourself out, take notes of the size of the pothole or obstruction and, if possible, photograph it. Councils have a convenient habit of filling in potholes as soon as they know an accident has taken place, so beat them to it with your camera.

If your crash involved another vehicle or person, swap details, and also try to see if anyone who saw the accident will give you their name and number. Witnesses can be very useful in litigation. Never admit you were at fault. It's not for you to decide.

If you are going to make an insurance claim – either for yourself or the bike — or think someone else has broken the law, tell the police. They will decide whether to prosecute.

If you are claiming on your insurance, brace yourself for a battle. Unlike in other countries, such as the Netherlands or Germany, UK law does not assume the innocence of the most vulnerable road user. Sadly, it is still the case that the cyclist must prove that he or she was in the right, rather than the other way round.

Your best bet is to join a cycling organization such as the CTC, which has legal experts who can help you with your claim. Third party insurance is included with CTC or British Cycling membership, which will protect you if you crash into someone else and are found liable for their costs.

EXAMPLE INSURANCE CLAIMS/PROSECUTIONS

Even if the accident is partially your fault, you could win compensation. In 2009, a schoolboy who sustained serious head injuries when he was hit by a car in Titchfield in Hampshire received compensation after a High Court hearing ruled that the driver who hit him was 50 per cent liable for the accident.

A cyclist won compensation after she rode on to the grass at the side of the road to avoid some loose gravel. Her bike hit a manhole cover on the verge, which was found to be the responsibility of British Telecom, and she fell, injuring her spine. This was a difficult claim because, initially, no local authority was prepared to take responsibility for the dangerous manhole cover. Despite this problem, her solicitors were able to prove negligent behaviour and successfully won the case.

Often the courts make bizarre decisions. In 2009, a man who killed a cyclist in County Durham while at the wheel of a car he was neither qualified nor insured to drive walked away from court with just a suspended sentence after the judge ruled that the cyclist's failure to wear a helmet was a 'mitigating factor' in his death.

A cyclist hurt in a hit and run accident in north west London in 2006 successfully recovered damages despite the driver never being traced. Liability for the accident was accepted by the Motor Insurers Bureau under the Untraced Driver's Agreement. The cyclist received compensation for his injuries and consequential losses and expenses.

CYCLING ETIQUETTE

It is very important to behave yourself on a bike. Not just so that other road users don't lamp you but because, if you don't, you'll give the rest of us a bad name. If we want the government to invest more funds into cycling facilities, we need to convince the non-cycling, tax-paying majority that we're not a bunch of reckless, smug idiots.

That said, is it ever acceptable to . . .

RUN RED LIGHTS?

Legally: no. The police can hit you with an on-the-spot fine of £30 if they catch you doing it. But people will always argue there are rational, sensible reasons for not waiting for the green light every now and again, though they may well have a job telling that to the judge.

Research shows red-light jumping is rampant. In 2009, academics from Hunter College in New York watched over 5,000 cyclists tackle 45 randomly generated intersections in Midtown Manhattan and found that 37 per cent of cyclists rode through red lights, while 28.7 per cent paused to look – then ran the light.

Red-light jumpers generally claim they only run the lights when it is safer to do so – or if it is late and there is no one around to see them err. They jump, they say, if they are caught up in the middle of traffic that will lurch as soon as the lights change, or if they are turning right across a box junction they know will not give them enough time to cross on green. Plus, some modern traffic lights – the ones which use induction loops buried under the tarmac which can change in your favour if they know you're there – aren't sensitive enough to register the presence of a light little cyclist, so you could be waiting for aeons on a quiet night if you don't run the red.

It is never, ever acceptable to run a red light at a pelican crossing where pedestrians are present. Ditto at a zebra crossing. Pedestrians are the most vulnerable road users, and they deserve to be able to cross the road at allotted places without you ploughing into them.

In August 2009, a British man was jailed for seven months after jumping on to a pavement to run a red light and killing an 84-year-old man.

. . . CYCLE WHILE TALKING ON
A MOBILE PHONE OR TEXTING?

It's not yet illegal in the UK, but it is pretty daft and you could be pulled over for a related offence of careless cycling. In the eyes of the law, it is illegal to use a mobile phone when driving a motor vehicle. There is nothing about bicycles in the phrasing so, in effect, cyclists are exempt from this. But cycle-texting and calling is rife. Before he became Mayor of London, and had to bite his tongue more often, Boris Johnson justified making calls on the road by suggesting that a ban on such behaviour was tantamount to discrimination: of one-armed people. What after all, is someone on their mobile phone, but a cyclist with one arm, was his logic.

. . . LISTEN TO AN IPOD WHILE CYCLING?

There is no law to stop you wearing headphones as you cycle, but it is about as clever as wearing sunglasses to drive in the dark. Though some of my nearest and dearest do this all the time, I can't bear it. You need to be able to hear what's coming in order to react to it. A number of people have been killed on their bikes while listening to MP3 players, with coroners specifically citing this as contributing to their deaths. If you must wear headphones while you cycle, you will need to compensate with even more visual checks over your shoulder than usual to see what's coming behind you.

. . . CYCLE WHEN DRUNK OR HIGH?

Legally, no. A person who cycles while unfit to ride through drink or drugs is guilty of an offence and can be fined up to £1,000 by magistrates. But if a police officer stops you, they cannot demand you take a breathalyser test or submit a urine sample. Instead, they have to establish your state by other means, such as asking you to walk in a straight line, or touch your nose with your eyes closed. In practice, however, unless you're doing something really reckless, they'll probably just tell you to get off your bike and walk it home. If they do this, resist the temptation to get back on it as soon as you round the corner. They'll be less sympathetic if they catch you further down the route.

Whether they admit it or not, most cyclists occasionally drink-cycle, though they would never consider getting behind the wheel of a car in the same condition. For many, one of the benefits of owning a bicycle is that they can save on a taxi fare home from the pub. Many people even own a 'pub bike' for this cheap purpose.

The truth is that riding a bicycle does require less concentration than driving, and the vast majority of people wobble home safely however full of booze they are. But accidents do happen. A good friend trashed his beloved racing bike ploughing into George IV Bridge in Edinburgh city centre after a particularly long day of drinking.

Another woke up in intensive care several days after leaving a pub lock-in. And what if you swerve into the road and cause a car accident?

A sobering statistic for you: in 2007, 55 per cent of cyclists aged sixteen or over killed while on their bikes had at least 80mg of alcohol per 100ml of blood, the legal limit for drink-driving, according to a 2008 government report on road casualties in Great Britain. Of course, this doesn't necessarily mean that the booze caused the accident, but it does tell you that it was perhaps a factor in what happened.

... BREAK THE SPEED LIMIT?

Speed limits only apply to motor vehicles. And even if a speed camera detected you whizzing past at 35mph in a built-up area, how on earth are they going to track you down?

However, you can be done for careless or dangerous cycling if you are deemed to have been cycling inappropriately quickly when you cause an accident. In 2009, a cyclist in Oxford was prosecuted for a careless cycling offence in the university town when he knocked down a thirteen-year-old boy. The cyclist admitted in court that his 15mph speed was too quick for the manoeuvre he was making, and he received a twelve-month conditional discharge and was ordered to pay £60 costs and £75 compensation.

'Dangerous cycling' – which is described in law as riding 'so that it would be obvious to a competent and careful cyclist that riding in that way would be dangerous' – carries a maximum fine of £2,500. You can be fined £1,000 for the lesser offence of riding a bike without due care and attention without reasonable consideration for others using the road.

... RIDE ON THE PAVEMENT?

No. Again, the police can and do issue Fixed Penalty Notices (FPN) of £30 a pop if they catch you doing it, though the law actually allows for a maximum fine of £500. If, however, you want your nine-year-old daughter to cycle to school, for example, and don't feel she is old enough to go on the road, she cannot be prosecuted even if there was a hardhearted enough copper out there willing to try. That's because, in England and Wales at least, the age of criminal responsibility begins at ten. But if you want to cycle with her, make sure you are in the road or you are breaking the law.

Quite apart from the legal issue, riding on the pavement is an arrogant and antisocial thing to do, and I hate seeing cyclists do it. Pedestrians deserve to feel safe on their bit of the street, so don't make them fight for it. If you are too wobbly to ride on the road, practise in the park until you've improved or, better still, get some cycle training from your local authority (more info to follow at the end of the chapter). Some pavement is specifically marked for shared use, but you should always give way to pedestrians.

. . . GO THE WRONG WAY
DOWN A ONE-WAY STREET?

Not unless it's a contraflow street where there is a bike lane marked going in the opposite direction to the motorized traffic. And even then, be careful – the facility is often badly signposted and drivers don't expect to see you coming towards them. Be especially mindful of pedestrians, who tend to only look in the direction of oncoming cars when crossing one-way streets. In London, in 2009, the borough of Kensington and Chelsea began a pilot scheme to allow cyclists to go against the flow on certain streets marked with a special 'No Entry – Except Cyclists' sign, but the results hadn't been published at the time of writing. NB: There is a special term for cyclists who ignore one-way signs, coined by the bitchy bike blogger Bike Snob NYC: bike salmon (think about it).

OTHER CRIMINAL OFFENCES

- ↘ Taking part in or organizing an unauthorized road race or time trial. This includes the 'alley cat' scavenger hunt type races popular among cycle couriers in big cities, where competitors race to reach a number of checkpoints in the fastest time
- ↘ Carrying passengers, unless your bike is a tandem or is otherwise designed to carry other people
- ↘ Ignoring traffic signs
- ↘ Refusing to give your name and address to a police officer when requested to do so
- ↘ There are also civil offences pertaining to cyclists, such as being sued by a farmer if you trespass on his land, or by another road user if you ride negligently and harm them or their property

HOW LIKELY AM I TO GET CAUGHT BREAKING THE LAW ON MY BIKE?

Not very. In 2007, 669 people were successfully prosecuted for 'offences involving a pedal cycle' in England and Wales. Just 26 of the guilty parties were women. Of those found guilty, 395 were given a fine, 114 were given a conditional discharge (i.e. they walked free on condition they didn't do anything bad for a prescribed period of time) and 48 got an absolute discharge (i.e. they were found officially guilty but given no punishment). In the same year, seven people were found guilty of offences involving a handcart or barrow, and 78 for crimes involving a horsedrawn vehicle. I tell you this for no other reason than it rather tickled me.

The government hasn't bothered breaking down the statistics for quite a few years, so we don't know what the most common cycling-related crimes and misdemeanours are. The last time they did, in 2003, 77 people were successfully prosecuted for 'careless/reckless' cycling, 82 for cycling on the pavement and 166 for 'lighting/ reflector offences'.

No one seems to know these days how likely you are to be issued with an on-the-spot fine for running red lights or cycling on the pavement, but in 1999 and 2000 the police issued respectively 665 and 821 Fixed Penalty Notices for cycling on the pavement, the only years for which these statistics were centrally collected. I've seen people getting hit with FPNs quite a few times, so be careful. If you get caught running a red light, having not seen the police watching, you are clearly nowhere near observant enough to be doing it safely.

COPING WITH BIKE RAGE

Though cycling has the potential to be a civilizing influence, it can also turn a mild-mannered pacifist into an aggressive crackpot. I've seen spitting, I've seen punching, I've been told I deserved to die. In *The Times*, Carol Midgley once told an astonishing story about being in a taxi and suddenly hearing loud bangs on the passenger door 'as if a randy bull was trying to mount it'. A scarlet-faced cyclist appeared and accused the taxi driver of driving too close. He may well have had a point. But what happened next went way beyond any acceptable expression of irritation: the cyclist scooped a fistful of gravel from his pocket and lobbed it at the cab, before making his escape. With horror, Midgley realized it was a pre-meditated attack. He had come armed for the job.

Worse things have happened. In April 2009, a rabid motorist in New Castle, Indiana, bit off a chunk of a cyclist's left ear after he complained about the car speeding. Sometimes the rage is from one cyclist to another. My friend got into such a fierce argument with another cyclist in the middle of a three lane road in south London that he forgot to look where he was going and slammed into a car. He woke up in hospital some hours later.

Don't be an angry cyclist. If someone puts you in danger, you have a right to let them know it is not acceptable, but try to rise above it. Being shouted at by motorists is, alas, one of the occupational hazards of cycling. But you don't have to shout back. Or bash your fist on their bonnet. Or deliberately scrape their paintwork. Don't be tempted to enter into any sort of stand-off. Cars are bigger, heavier and much faster than bikes and you will never win. Keep calm and carry on.

CYCLE TRAINING

If you are wobbly on your bike after decades away from the saddle, it is worth signing up for some cycle training and gaining your Bikeability badge. This is not nearly as lame as it sounds – I did a session while researching this book and picked up some useful titbits. The instructor pointed out I have a tendency to cower in the kerb, am not very good at emergency stops and always forget to change down a gear when at traffic lights.

Right into the new millennium, only children were given cycling lessons in preparation for that rite of passage, the cycling proficiency test. But nowadays, adults can also receive tuition as part of the new National Standard for Cycle Training, which sets out the skills needed for cyclists to be competent and confident using their bikes for all sorts of journeys. You will be taught the Bikeability syllabus, which is in three stages, starting gently by learning to handle your bike properly (using gears and brakes), right up to entering busy multi-lane roads.

If you did the cycling proficiency, you'll no doubt remember a lot of weaving in and out of cones in the playground and reacting to imaginary scenarios. Nowadays, cycle training is road based, and instructors will take you out on to real roads to practise the skills you need to cycle safely. They are particularly useful for nervous cyclists or those who are out of practice.

Training can cost from £15 per person per session, depending on your geographical location. Many local authorities fund courses that are free or subsidized. Contact your local training provider or independent National Standard cycle instructor for details of their charging policy. See also www.bikeability.org.uk

KEEPING
YOUR
BIKE
YOURS

It was a lovely summer's day, and I was enjoying my four-mile commute into central London even more than usual when there was a sudden thud as the rim of my rear wheel hit a speed bump. Flat tyre. I looked at my watch: twenty minutes until morning conference. I was going to have to abandon my wounded steed and hop on a bus if I was to make it in on time. I spotted a set of railings running along the busy bus route, secured my bike using the two locks I always carry and flagged down the number 55.

As I returned that evening, armed with a spare inner tube, tyre levers and pump, my only concern was whether I'd be able to mend the puncture all by myself. I needn't have worried. When I arrived, there was no puncture to mend, because some sod had stolen my bicycle. Somehow, the fact they had nicked a sickly bike made it worse. It was like mugging a blind person, or swindling an impoverished pensioner out of her winter fuel allowance.

I couldn't even allow myself a momentary delusion – was I looking in the wrong place? – because shackled to the railings was my front wheel, the pristine one with an unpunctured tyre. I was furious with myself. Why had I used my best lock, the £70 D-lock that weighs me down every day, to secure just my front wheel, and the flimsy £20 number to wrap around the far more expensive frame and rear wheel?

Wiping away tears, I unlocked my orphaned wheel and walked with it forlornly to Bethnal Green police station. 'Look!' I told the woman behind the counter, red-eyed, as I showed her what was left of my beautiful bicycle, the £500 racer I had bought just two months earlier to cycle from London to Land's End. She barely looked up. I knew then I would never see my baby again. I never really got over it. Like a jilted lover who refuses to take down pictures of the one they lost, I kept the front wheel in my flat as a reminder of what had so cruelly been taken away from me.

What makes this episode so infuriating is that within eighteen months that lonely front wheel had been joined in my hallway by the skeleton of my next bike – another nimble racer, which I had bought on the insurance and loved with frightening intensity. Theft number two proved I hadn't learned my lesson. I left it outside a dodgy late licence pub in Hackney, naively assuming that as I'd parked it right opposite the bouncers it would be fine. But when I eventually left, I couldn't believe what I saw. Surely that mournful Trek bike frame dangling from the rack by an expensive-looking D-lock wasn't the frame from my Trek bike? Where were the wheels? The seat? The bloody handlebars! Like a wartime village, my bike had been pillaged. I wept. I couldn't believe it had happened again.

I learned an important lesson that night. It's a shame my then boyfriend didn't. He borrowed bike number three, yet another agile racer paid for by my insurance company, 'just to nip to Tesco Metro'. He ignored my instructions to always, always secure the back wheel and frame with the £70 D-lock. My bike and I weren't the only things that parted company that night.

Rare is the regular cyclist who hasn't had a bike stolen at some point. In 2008/9, a staggering 540,000 bicycles were stolen in Britain, according to the British Crime Survey – a 22 per cent increase on the previous year. The really irritating thing is that, despite the astonishing number of bike thefts, the police hardly ever catch the thieves. I don't think they even try. In 2007, just 1,173 people were successfully prosecuted for stealing bikes according to the UK government's Criminal Statistics annual report. The figures show that the culprits are nearly always men; of those found guilty just thirty were women.

When I tell people another bike has gone, they often ask me why I keep getting nice bikes. Why not buy a cheaper, secondhand number for razzing around town and, if I really must, keep an expensive one in the flat for weekend adventuring? Though this solution may result in less heartache, take umbrage at it. For me, the joy of bicycling has a lot to do with riding a machine I love. I like it to be nippy and light and look nice. Why spend most of my cycling time on a clunky machine I'm loath to be seen on? If no one wants to steal it, it's because they don't think anyone else would like to ride it, so why should I? If you buy a rubbish bike, chances are you'll rarely use it, and what's the point in that? On a similar note, I refuse to disguise mine by making it ugly with gaffer tape or that ridiculous fake rust you can buy (see http://www.dominicwilcox.com/stickers.html), though many people swear by this uglification tactic.

And anyway, cycle theft is not inevitable – follow the instructions in this chapter and, Insha'Allah, your bike will remain yours.

WHICH LOCK?

A good one. Ideally two, especially if you live in a big city where bike theft is rife. You're generally told to spend at least 10 per cent of the cost of your bike on a lock, but buying anything under £40 is a waste of money unless you're going to use it as your secondary lock (just to secure your front wheel). Several thieves have tried and failed to break my £70 Abus D-lock. The woman who sold it to me said she had never heard of anyone having their bike stolen when using it properly.

Apart from cost, the other bad news is that the best locks are also the heaviest. It is a cruel truth that in order to thwart a thief trying to pinch your featherlight carbon-framed beauty, you will have to arm yourself with a lock that weighs more than the bike. Sorry about that. While I am delivering bad tidings, I might as well warn you that no lock is tough enough to withstand a really determined attack. If a thief wants your bike and is given more than five minutes to do so then he (it's usually a he, remember) will take it. The git.

Remember when buying a lock to choose one that isn't too big for your frame if you want to attach it using a holster. You can buy holsters for most of the big-name locks if you don't have one or have lost or broken yours, though they tend to be scandalously expensive for what they are. Most bike shops will be happy to fit them for you if you struggle. Your lock should also not be so small that it won't go around your bike and an immovable object.

Once you have a lock, oil it a little every now and again to stop it sticking. If you do leave your bike outside for a prolonged period and the lock has seized up, often squirting in some WD-40 or similar and leaving for a few minutes will do the trick.

D-LOCKS
[AKA U-LOCKS]

For your primary, don't-even-think-about-stealing-this-you-hoodlum lock, choose a sturdy D-lock.

Buy the most expensive one you can afford and always use it to lock the dearest bits of your bike, i.e. the frame and back wheel. You may recall the famous video showing someone picking a D-lock with a Biro. Old news. New models don't have the same flaw and, anyway, picking locks is a bit Victorian. Most modern bike thieves prefer brute force and heavy equipment to simply break or cut through locks. D-locks are best because they are solid and have no weak links. Buy the smallest D-lock that works for you, because you want as little space as possible between the lock, the bike and whatever you are locking it to.

If you've ever wondered why you see so many D-locks hanging from bike stands with no bicycle in sight, it is not because someone has picked the lock, stolen the bike and left the lock to goad the victim. It's almost always because the lock belongs to a commuter who leaves their bike in the same spot every day and doesn't want to cart the lock to and from work. This is a silly thing to do – not only does it tell a thief that your bike will be in a predictable place for a predictable period of time every day, but it also gives them a chance to work on your lock while your bike is not there so they can steal it with ease when it is.

If you have quick-release wheels and only want to carry one lock, you could take off the front wheel and lock it to the back wheel and frame, but I find it too messy and fiddly.

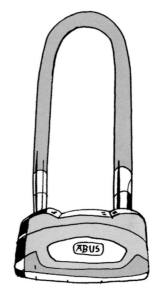

↘ D-locks

CHAIN LOCKS

After a D-lock, your next best option is a chunky chain lock.

↘ chain lock

Problem is, good chain locks are incredibly heavy. Their advantage is that they are flexible, and so easier to attach to stout lampposts and to carry (you can put them around your waist or shoulders). But the links can be vulnerable to chiselling. Be vigilant if your chain lock has a cover over it, as it can disguise any pre-emptive sawing. Thieves are known to pull back the cover, saw away at the chain until it is almost broken, then put the cover back on. That way, when you arrive the following day, you won't notice anything awry, but the thieves can swipe your bike in seconds by quickly sawing away at the link they have prepared earlier.

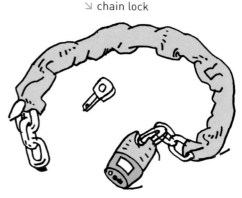

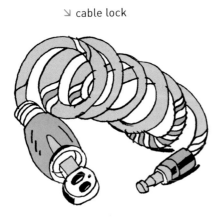
↘ cable lock

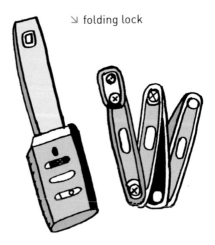
↘ folding lock

CABLE LOCKS

Cable locks are generally much lighter and more portable, but never use them for anything other than attaching your front wheel to your frame (to stop thieves opening the quick release and running off with it) and for securing other things, such as your seat and bottle cage. Two of my beloved bicycles were stolen while 'secured' with one of these.

FOLDING LOCKS

An alternative to a cable lock is a folding lock. These are very portable and can fit around awkward shaped objects. They are handy, but not really strong enough to use as your primary lock.

There is a good video called 'Lock it or lose it' on the http://quickrelease.tv/ website

OTHER SECURITY MEASURES

IMMOBILIZERS

This is a device attached to your bike which locks the back wheel, making it impossible to ride. They are often fitted on Dutch bikes, but should not be relied on for anything more than very quick stops where your bike is in full view.

LOCKING NUTS, CODED ALLEN KEYS, CODED SECURITY SKEWERS

If you are fed up with thieves stealing bits of your bike, consider fitting these secure alternatives to quick-release or standard nuts and bolts. They can be used to clamp forks, saddle, wheels and handlebars and are a good alternative to a second lock. They are easy to install and use – just don't lose the key. For wheels, they're often more hassle than they're worth, as you'll have to carry the keys around with you in case you get a puncture and need to take the wheel off.

SOLD SECURE

When buying a lock in the UK, look for a Sold Secure rating. Sold Secure is an independent test laboratory established by Northumbria and Essex Police and the Home Office and now run by the not-for-profit Master Locksmiths Association. They test security products and award them ratings according to how effective they are. The gold-rated locking devices offer the highest level of security, and can withstand at least five minutes of attack with a full set of tools. Silver offers a compromise between security and cost, while the bronze level typically just offers defence against the opportunist thief. You can search on their website to see which products they have tested: www.soldsecure.com

It is also worth looking out for the German and Dutch standards, ART1 and 5+. Gold or high ART-rated locks can be more expensive, but it may help you get a discount on your insurance if you use one.

ANTI-THEFT GUARANTEE

Some locks come with a guarantee promising to buy you a new bike if a thief cracks your lock. It is often difficult to claim this, however, as you have to prove the lock was broken by sending them the remains, and often bike thieves leave no trace.

WARRANTY

Some lock manufacturers offer warranties to replace the lock if your cycle is stolen while locked with their product. You may have to register and/or pay for the service and, again, you will likely have to prove the lock was broken.

THE DO'S AND DON'TS OF LOCKING YOUR BIKE

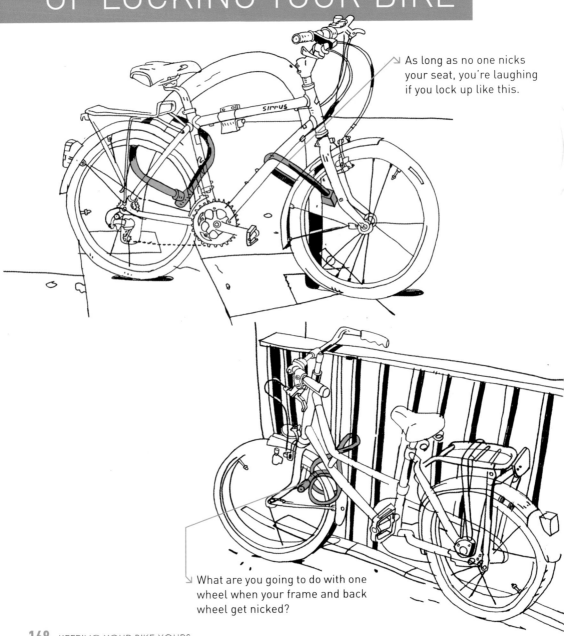

As long as no one nicks your seat, you're laughing if you lock up like this.

What are you going to do with one wheel when your frame and back wheel get nicked?

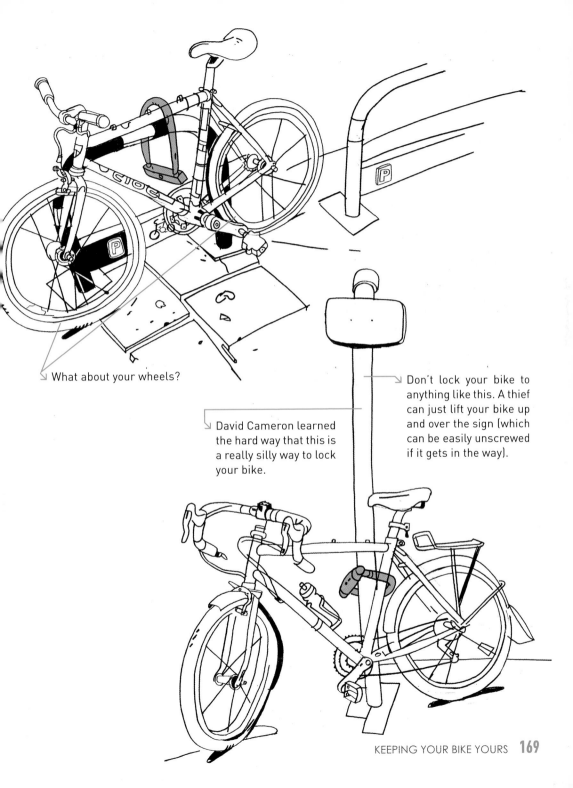

What about your wheels?

David Cameron learned the hard way that this is a really silly way to lock your bike.

Don't lock your bike to anything like this. A thief can just lift your bike up and over the sign (which can be easily unscrewed if it gets in the way).

OTHER THIEF-THWARTING TACTICS

- ↘ Never leave your bike unlocked. So many people get caught out just nipping into the corner shop to buy a paper.

- ↘ Lock your bike somewhere public, but remember that a busy place doesn't necessarily equal a safe place. Once, I had to saw off a frozen lock right outside a bustling tube station and not one person stopped and asked what I was up to.

- ↘ Never lock your bike up somewhere quiet and out of the way where a thief can work undisturbed. Five minutes is the maximum a thief will generally spend on a job, unless you make it easy for them.

- ↘ Don't lock your bike somewhere that makes it obvious you won't be back for some time (outside a cinema is the classic example). Even just going fifty yards down the road and locking it outside a restaurant is a far safer option.

- ↘ Make the lock mechanism hard to reach.

- ↘ Never lock your bike to something easier to break than a lock – don't use a young tree or wooden fence as an anchor.

- ↘ Don't leave a commuting lock on railings or bike racks – thieves can practise on it when you're not around and break it when your bike's in it.

- ↘ Use your bike and stand to fill the space within your lock, as any slack can be exploited.

- ↘ Lock low down to make rotational leverage harder, but keep your lock off the ground so thieves have nothing to strike against. If your chain is on the floor, a thief can easily chisel it until it cracks open.

- ↘ Don't lock close to a wall or other hard object which will help thieves by giving them something to lean against when they put the crowbar in.

- ↘ If you can only lock one wheel, make it the rear one. It is far cheaper to replace the front one.

- ↘ Lock your bike next to a nicer-looking model, or at least one with a flimsier lock.

- ↘ Never leave any tools on your bike. My beloved left a set of Allen keys in his saddlebag while he went swimming, and when he came out a thief had helped himself to both his saddle and that belonging to the neighbouring bike. The owner of the other bike was not amused.

- ↘ If you're using two locks, choose two different kinds. Thieves often only carry one tool for a particular kind of lock.

- ↘ If you have a fancy saddle, or any quick-release one that can be undone without tools, loop a cable lock through it.

- ↘ Remove all the bits and bobs – lights, bike computers, panniers, bottles, etc.

- Make sure you know where the spare keys to the locks are.
- When you get a new bike, write down the frame number (it's usually either underneath the bottom bracket by the pedals or on the rear fork ends where the back wheel slots in) and register it with the police via a site such as www.bikeregister.com or www.immobilise.com. Also consider photographing your bike with a note of the model number and any other significant details that might help the police recover your bike.

The world's most prolific bike thief?

When Canadian police arrested bike-shop owner Igor Kenk in July 2008, they discovered 2,865 stolen bicycles squirrelled away in various garages across Toronto.

Kenk, a 49-year-old former judo champion from Latvia who ran a small bike shop in Toronto city centre, was accused of either personally stealing or arranging to have stolen this astonishing haul. He was caught when police saw him allegedly instructing a mentally ill man to cut the locks on two bicycles.

Rounding up his ill-gotten gains took an enormous police operation. They raided fourteen lock-ups, as well as his bike shop, all of which were packed to the rafters with bicycles of unknown provenance.

It took days for police to sort through the tangled mountain of bikes. They eventually lined them up, wheels in the air, in an unused factory and police garage, and invited members of the public to come along and search for their long-lost machines. By Christmas 2008, police had returned 573 of the seized bikes to their owners, some of whom wept at the reunion.

Kenk's arrest was a long time coming. He was well known to police, and for years his shop was the first port of call for many cyclists after their bikes had been stolen. Often, these victims were able to recover them, either through vigorous argument or a payment of CAN$30 or CAN $40 (£17 or £23).

In court, Kenk never showed remorse for the pain he had caused his victims, nor gave any indication what on earth he was planning to do with his 2,865-strong collection. But according to one of his former acquaintances, Kenk got into bike theft when his own treasured mountain bike was stolen. He reported it to the police, but it was never recovered, one of his former friends told the *Toronto Star* newspaper. 'He was devastated,' said Polly, owner of another Toronto bike shop. 'That kind of really messed him up.' After striking a plea bargaining deal with prosecutors in December 2009, Kenk eventually pleaded guilty to just ten counts of theft and was sentenced to thirty months in jail – roughly one day behind bars for every three bikes he was alleged to have stolen.

SAFE STORAGE SOLUTIONS

ANCHORS

These extra-strong, hardened braces are anchored on to the floor or wall with long, sturdy fastening elements you lock your bike to. Ideally, fit these in a shed or a garage with solid walls or floors.

LOCKERS

You can buy metal lockers such as the Bike Bunker (www.cycle-works.com) or Protect-A-Cycle (www.protectacycle.co.uk), which are designed to hold a small number of bicycles outside your house.

CYCLOC

This nifty little wall-mounted device is perfect if you have a small flat and need to get your bike out of the hallway. At the time of writing, the Cycloc only fitted bikes with a top tube (crossbar), but the designer promised a model for ladies' bikes would soon be available: www.cycloc.com

PULLEY SYSTEM

If your hallway has dead space above head height, you could try to install a pulley system of the type used to dry washing in the olden days. You can buy a bicycle-specific hoist for around £20.

PLANTLOCK

If you can't keep your bike indoors, these rather beautiful flower tubs offer something secure to lock your bike to. Once you've filled it with soil and plants, the PlantLock weighs 75+kg and provides safe and tidy bike storage. You can install them wherever you like – in your garden, on your balcony or patio. Each PlantLock accommodates two bicycles and is available in a range of colours. Made by www.frontyardcompany.co.uk

SHELTERS

If you have the space, you could install a covered bicycle store for use out-doors. These are generally made from a metal frame covered with canvas, and should usually be used in conjunction with a wall or floor anchor. Examples include the BikePort (www.frontyardcompany.co.uk) and the Bike Cave (www.tidytent.com)

IMPROVISED SOLUTIONS

If you live in a block of flats and the management company or freeholder is too pig-headed to sort you out with secure bike storage, improvise. Some time ago, everyone in my building received a snotty letter warning that if we didn't move bikes from communal corridors they would be removed without notice, as they were a fire hazard. We were outraged, especially as we had all written to the company on many occasions asking for them to make provisions for bicycles. There was nothing for it but to take matters into our own hands and my enterprising neighbour Toby hauled a concrete block up to our floor, with two heavy-duty chains bolted to each end. One was for me, one for him and his family. If the overlords have attempted to remove our bikes at any point since, they certainly haven't managed it.

INSURANCE

If your bike is worth more than £200, it is really worth insuring it. My long-suffering insurance company paid out for three brand-new bikes in three years (plus new locks, lights, etc) after they were stolen. Often, you can extend your household contents insurance to include a bike for free (or a minimal fee), though this rarely covers any bike over £500, and the excess might be excessive. The insurance on my flat, in a not particularly desirable part of east London, was only £150 including the bike, so it was well worth it. When I came to renew the cover after the third theft, however, the premium and excess had shot up massively, and I decided to get specific bike insurance separately.

INSURANCE TIPS

- When estimating how much your bike is worth be sure to include the cost of all the accessories permanently fixed to it. They can easily add on £100.
- Bear in mind that certain conditions may be attached to your policy. Some insurers insist that you use a specific grade of lock and may request proof, so it's a good idea to keep receipts.
- Some insurers will not pay up if your bike is stolen from a communal hallway.
- Check what the insurers are offering. Some will only reimburse you the cost of your bike when you bought it. The best policies offer 'new-for-old'.
- Some insurers will pay for your taxi home if you find yourself stranded after a theft.
- Many insurers offer no-claims protection, which protects your no-claims bonus even if you make a claim and leaves your insurance premium clean. This is an especially good idea if you live somewhere dodgy and think bike theft is inevitable.
- If you are going to be doing any racing, make sure your policy will cover you.
- Check if you're covered when taking your bike abroad.
- Some insurers will not pay out if you are deemed to have abandoned your bike. This can mean leaving it locked but unattended for as little as twelve hours.
- If you are insuring a secondhand bike, make sure you have evidence that you bought it from a reputable seller. Ideally, keep their name, address and VAT number on record.

- Beware when lending out your bike that some insurers will only pay out if you were the one who locked it up when it was stolen. Others will cover immediate family but not friends, including live-in partners.
- Insurers are often very fussy about where you leave bicycles at stations. Most stipulate that you must only use a rack 'supplied by the train station expressly for the purpose of securing bikes, and within the jurisdiction of the transport police'.
- If you leave your bike indoors, make sure it is not on public display in a window. Many insurers will not pay up if the building is broken into and they deem that your bike was not stored out of sight.

EXTRA SECURITY MEASURES

SECURITY MARKING

Sometimes it will be a condition of your insurance policy to get your bike security tagged. This can take many forms. Some police stations will stamp your postcode and house number or name on to your bike and keep an electronic record of your details. They will also give you a coded cycle sticker to show that it has been marked, which might in itself deter a thief. If you'd rather go DIY, you could also use an ultra-violet pen to write your name or address on the bike.

DATA TAGGING

Another option is to fit an electronic tag and corresponding record kept on a database with a system such as Datatag (www.datatag.co.uk). The Datatag is tiny and fits inside the frame of your bike, and is detectable by the police. According to the company which makes the device, the Crown Prosecution Service has a 100 per cent successful prosecution rate when evidence has been supplied by Datatag. The kit, which costs around £25, includes both visible and hidden identifiers, including a Datatag transponder that gives your bike a unique electronic fingerprint.

BUT IF YOUR BIKE IS STOLEN . . .

Always report it to the police. You can either do this in person, on the phone or online. Don't hold your breath that they'll find your bike, but it is important that they have accurate figures on how widespread bike theft is, if nothing else. Give them as much information as you can, including the frame number, type of bike, any distinctive details, where and when it was stolen and, if you can, a photo. If you're thinking straight when you notice that your bike has been swiped, check around to see if there are any CCTV cameras, private or public, and tell the police if there are. Make sure you are given a crime reference number, which you will need to provide to your insurance company. For some insurers, this is enough, but others require you to send off the key to your lock.

If you are unlucky enough to be mugged for your bike (a rare occurrence; don't panic), police recommend you don't put up a fight but surrender your bike and call 999 as soon as you can.

It is always worth keeping an eye on eBay and Gumtree and similar websites in the days, weeks and even months after your bike goes missing. Thieves are sometimes thick/complacent enough to advertise their wares online. If you think you have found a listing for your bike, tell the police immediately. Sometimes sad stories have happy endings: in 2009, a man called Paul Jones was reunited with his £1,400 bike a year after it had been stolen in Bristol. Straight after the theft, Jones had posted intimate details about the bike on various internet forums and, twelve months later, eagle-eyed members of one fixed gear forum discovered the bike for sale on eBay. Avon and Somerset police recovered it the same day, and even delivered it to his home.

A cautionary tale

Before you call the police, do make sure that your bike really is stolen. Once, when I first moved to London, I was on my way to work when I realized I needed new batteries for my Dictaphone. I locked my bike to a lamp-post, nipped into a shop and came out five minutes later to discover, to my absolute horror, that my bike had vanished. Having heard about the bike theft epidemic in the capital, I had long expected the inevitable, and now it had happened. I blinked away tears and called the police. That night, I was too depressed to face the long bus ride home, so treated myself to a taxi. I decided to torture myself by making the driver take a route which involved returning to the scene of the crime. I looked out of the window like a mournful puppy as we approached the spot. I expected a surge of sadness in my belly, but what I saw made my heart leap. My bike was still there! Shackled to the lamp-post where I had left it. Not the one 50 yards up where I had looked in vain for it. When the policewoman called the following day to check details, I told her I had found my bike. I didn't think she needed to know the details.

CYCLING TO WORK

One of the many soul-destroying things about the world of work is the commute. Whether it's being stuck in heavy traffic, waiting endlessly for buses that never materialize or being thrust under someone else's foetid armpit on an overcrowded train, the journey has the potential to spoil even the most perfect of days.

No wonder an increasing number of people are choosing to cycle to work. Not long ago, most right-thinking people wouldn't countenance such an idea – commuting by bicycle was for dishevelled outcasts with poor personal hygiene and perennially crumpled clothing. It is no coincidence that the main character in The 40 Year Old Virgin is a bike commuter. During one of his many failed attempts to get his leg over, the object of his affection cites 'and you CYCLE to work!' as the ultimate example of why he has yet to make love to a woman.

Happily, things have changed, and cycling to work is no longer the preserve of the unironed, unwashed and enduringly unerotic few. Though it takes a little bit of forward planning, these days, all sorts of people commute by bike and turn up smelling fresh and looking smart, having carried with them their laptops, papers and all the other bits and bobs they need. The government has even introduced tax breaks to help them do it.

Before we get to that, though, we need to address all the excuses you'll no doubt come up with when persuading yourself that you couldn't possibly commute by bicycle.

EXCUSES, EXCUSES

I DON'T HAVE THE RIGHT BIKE

There's no such thing as the 'right' bike. If you have a roadworthy bicycle, you can cycle to work on it, whether it's an old rustbucket you found in the shed or a souped-up racing bike you usually only pose with on the weekends. There is a mad man in London who cycles to work every day on a unicycle, wearing a fluorescent vest and helmet. But if you want to buy a commuter bike, look for one with a more upright riding position and a way of transporting luggage (a rack or basket or handlebars capable of carrying a bag), and mudguards and perhaps a chain or skirt guard to keep your clothes clean. See chapter 1 for which bikes work best for commuting.

IT'S TOO DANGEROUS

Though the authorities could do far more to make cycling safer, you don't need a death wish to cycle, especially if you design a quiet route away from major thoroughfares. Often non-cyclists perceive cycling to be far more dangerous than it really is because they don't tend to travel on bike-friendly roads. People who get the bus to work tell their cycling colleagues they must be mad to commute by bike because they look out of the bus window, see kamikaze cyclists squeezing through minuscule gaps in the traffic and think 'Not for me, mate.' The fact that bicycle commuters are always told how 'brave' they are doesn't really help either.

Many novice bike commuters make the mistake of taking the same route on their bicycle as they would in their car or on public transport. That's how they end up sandwiched between buses on Edinburgh's Princes Street or gasping for air on the Oxford Road in Manchester. Most local authorities have drawn up maps showing the most cycle-friendly routes in the area, and local cycling organizations will also be more than happy to help you plot a safe journey. If you check on their websites, you'll see many have used Google Maps to plot bike-friendly routes, showing bike shops, accident blackspots and more.

If you are thinking of starting to cycle to work, ask your colleagues for tips on the quietest routes in. I sometimes plot non-scary commutes for friends using the very handy Gmaps Pedometer (http://www.gmap-pedometer.com) – you can save the URL and forward it on.

If cycling down a big road is unavoidable, make sure that you are visible, and don't cycle in the gutter. Though it sounds paradoxical, the closer you are to the kerb, the more likely cars are to pass you at scary proximity.

Route-finding tools

↘ The Cycle Maps website features a handy directory of all online cycle maps in England, Scotland, Wales and Northern Ireland.
www.cyclemaps.org.uk

↘ Cycle Streets is a UK-wide cycle journey planner system, which lets you plan routes by bike. You can opt to search for the quietest or quickest route, and if you tell it how fast you plan to cycle, it'll estimate your arrival time. It also shows where the traffic lights and crossings are, as well as bike shops and toilets, and warns you if you'll have to get off your bike anywhere along the way. Photos of many streets have also been uploaded, so you can check out just how many bike racks there are at your destination or whether those lights will let you turn right.
www.cyclestreets.net

↘ Transport Direct, a clever not-for-profit website which offers information for door-to-door travel for both public transport and car journeys, includes a cycle route planner. At the time of writing, the site only covered ten cities/regions, but there are plans to extend its reach. It allows you to dictate the maximum speed at which you would like to travel, choose to avoid unlit roads, walking with your bike, or steep climbs, and gives you a graph showing the gradient of your route. It is also compatible with most modern PDAs and mobile phones.
www.transportdirect.info

↘ Bikely is an international community website where cyclists can share their routes.
www.bikely.com

↘ In London, the Transport for London website has a not-bad online route planner for cyclists. Click the 'additional cycling options' box underneath the bit where it asks you to specify which forms of transport you want to search for, and you can tell it that you want to be able to leave your bike at a station, or take it with you on public transport, as well as stipulate how long you are prepared to cycle for.
http://journeyplanner.tfl.gov.uk

I'LL SMELL

If you don't already have a body odour problem, cycling is not going to make you develop one. Yes, you probably will sweat more commuting by bike than you would sitting on the bus, but this is not an insurmountable problem. There are many precautions you can take to ensure you don't become the person no one wants to sit next to in the office.

First of all, you can simply cycle slowly, wearing layers you can discard as you warm up. You are going from home to your workplace. It is not a race. You wouldn't run to work and expect to turn up immaculate, so resist the temptation to pedal as fast as you can, at least on the way in. You can always bomb it on the way home and let those you live with suffer the consequences.

Remember, too, that going, say, 10mph instead of 12mph isn't going to make all that much difference on a short commute, particularly in urban areas, where you'll have to stop at traffic lights every few minutes (or at least you ought to be stopping). It is an underrated pleasure being overtaken by cyclists who seem to have mistaken their commute for the Tour de France only to sidle up alongside them coolly while they are panting, frustrated and knackered at the lights.

Still, many people cannot bear not going at full throttle in both directions, either because they're always late, they like the exercise or they simply can't bear being overtaken. If you are one of these people, I would advise you not to wear your work clothes on the commute. You should probably carry at least a different top to change out of on arrival, otherwise you may well pollute the office air and become the person everyone else circulates bitchy emails about.

It is also worth remembering that, in warm weather, although you might not think you are perspiring at all while pedalling along, you may well break out into a sweat once you stop. That's because, when you're on the move, the air cools you nicely, but not when you're stationary. If you're being organized enough, try to factor in five minutes at the end of your commute to cool down. Otherwise, even if you shower and get changed, you could end up sweating on your clean gear.

If you want to cycle in clothes that can't be machine-washed, wear a vest or petticoat underneath. It might sound a little wartime, but you'll really save on dry cleaning bills.

MY WORKPLACE DOESN'T HAVE A SHOWER

If you don't have showers at your workplace, but want to freshen up on arrival, you have a few options. You could have a wash in the sink – but if there aren't private basins in individual cubicles, you might feel a bit self-conscious soaping your armpits when the boss walks in to do their thing.

A more dignified option would be to carry baby wipes, which you can easily use in the toilet stall. I carry baby wipes in my saddlebag along with my puncture repair kit, and they're tremendously useful in all sorts of circumstances. When I'm being lazy and can't be bothered giving my bike a proper wash – which involves carrying it down two flights of stairs to a very public patch of grass generally surrounded by a gang of sarcastic youths – I give it a sort of bed bath in my corridor with baby wipes. Works a treat and doesn't ruin the carpet.

With the baby-wipe option, do shower before you leave the house in the morning. That way, any sweat you do produce while pedalling will be fresh and untainted by the bacteria that makes you smell like a meat pie.

You could also try to find a gym or sports centre nearby with affordable shower facilities, but this generally works out pretty expensive, unless you actually want to do some activities there as well. Some friendly bike shops in New York have showers and bike parking spaces, though the idea has yet to catch on much elsewhere.

You also have the option of using a 'shower in a bottle' such as Rocket Shower. This product, comprising mostly witch hazel and alcohol, is for use after you've cooled down and stopped sweating actively. You spray yourself down with it, then towel yourself dry, and the believers swear it removes that sticky salty feeling and leaves your skin feeling dry and refreshed. That's the theory, anyway – I tried it and found it surprisingly effective during a rare British heatwave. You can buy it in various online bike shops or via the website: www.10nine8.net

There is, of course, also the teenage option of taking what my xenophobic classmates and I used to call a 'French shower', and simply douse your-self in deodorant. But that would be gross.

MINE DOES, BUT SHOULD I BOTHER?

If your work does have a shower, lucky you. At least you have the option. Using it regularly does require a bit of advance planning, however, as you'll probably need a locker to keep your wash bag, as well as somewhere to hang and dry your towel afterwards. And what if you need to dry your hair?

In my opinion, unless you are a really heavy perspirer and/or have to cycle a dreadfully long way, a shower isn't really necessary in ordinary weather. Most bicycle commuters choose simply to change into fresh work clothes instead. It's not that big a deal, and there are some clever bags and panniers available now that will keep your clothes crumple-free (more of which later).

MY WORK CLOTHES WILL GET OILY AND GRUBBY

This is true. They might. But not if you're careful and cycle gently, or choose to cycle in old clothes and get changed on arrival. If you want to cycle in your work clothes, you can minimize the chances of looking a complete state by choosing a bike that goes out of its way to keep you clean. Upright, Dutch-style bicycles are generally the best for this, but you should just look for anything with mudguards and a chain guard and perhaps also a skirt protector, which covers the top half of your back wheel and will stop your skirt or coat getting caught in the spokes and gear hub. This will keep all of the bike's oily bits well away from your bottom half, and minimize the splash from muddy puddles. Single speed bikes – or those with hub gears, which do not have sticky-out cogs – are good from the point of view of you staying clean.

Try to avoid wearing a rucksack, as it's a fast track to a seriously sweaty back. It will also give you a sore neck.

Before I got a Dutch bike, I commuted four miles to my office and back on a racing bike with none of the above as standard, and I still cycled in my work gear unless it was really hot or raining violently, or I was wearing something totally inappropriate like a pencil skirt. I have temporary 'racing' mudguards I can clip easily to my bike should rain be forecast (see chapter 2, bike accessories) and carry a cagoule should the weather turn. I keep a smart coat at the office in case I need to go out, as I don't want to be seen as the sort of person who thinks a cagoule is acceptable attire when not cycling or fell walking.

I have simply tailored my workwear to be as bike-friendly as possible, and in the winter can usually be seen in opaque black tights (totally oil-proof), boots and an array of dresses in either stretchy material or with a more flared skirt. I do have a weakness for 1940s dresses, however, which are all far too fitted around the hips for cycling in. The days I feel like dressing up as Barbara Stanwyck, I cycle to work in capri pants or leggings and a vest and change on arrival. For more tips on looking chic on a bike, see chapter 3.

WHAT IF IT RAINS?

Either don rain gear, or leave the bike at home. No shame in that. Incidentally, I am very fond of this joyously simple website, which gives you the probability of it raining wherever you are the following day: http://isitgoingtoraintomorrow.com

I ALWAYS WEAR HEELS AT WORK

Fine. Cycle in them if you like, though I prefer keeping a pair under my desk to change into on arrival. If you are going to cycle in impractical shoes, bear in mind that you will probably go a lot slower than in sturdy flats, because of a physics equation involving force and surface area. I really wouldn't advise commuting in heels in bad weather, as they tend to have very slippery soles which will slide off wet pedals. See p.88 for a discussion of this dilemma.

I DON'T WANT MY COLLEAGUES TO SEE ME IN MY CYCLING SHORTS

Don't wear them, then. Or hide them underneath a more socially acceptable garment and no one ever need know. Or just rush to the toilets to get changed the minute you arrive. You can always do it in a nearby café if you can't even risk being spotted in the staff toilets. Just don't be one of those weirdos wearing cycle gear for too long in an inappropriate setting. Gentlemen, remember: the further you are away from your bike while wearing Lycra, the more you will look like a pervert.

MY SHIRT WILL GET CRUMPLED

Not if you fold it properly, it won't. Get into the habit of folding it neatly like a shop assistant, and if you can be bothered (though I bet you can't), wrap it in tissue paper, and you'll be fine. If you have somewhere at work to hang clothes, you could always take in a load of shirts on a Monday via public transport or in the car to see you through the week. You can, of course, also buy non-iron shirts, but I've yet to see any that survive being stuffed into a pannier willy nilly.

I HAVE TO WEAR A SUIT

This is not a disaster. The first pioneering cyclists always rode in neat suits, stiff-collared shirts and peaked caps. If you've not got far to go, the best option is simply to wear it. Many of the Hasidic Jews near me cycle in their long black tailcoats, crisp white shirts and big furry hats. Boris Johnson always bikes in a suit, and I've never heard anyone complaining about his body odour. He does, however, look perennially dishevelled, so if you want to avoid the I-slept-in-this look, carry your suit in a suit carrier.

Highson (www.highson.co.uk) makes a waterproof jacket that also incorporates a removable suit carrier which straps to the wearer's back. Though clever, it will make you resemble a cagoule-wearing hunchback, which isn't a look for everyone. And the Canadian website Two Wheel Gear (www.twowheelgear.com) sells a well-regarded suit carrying pannier and ships to Canada, the US, the UK, Australia and Japan.

You could also buy special 'packing folders' designed to slip inside another bag, and which claim to keep clothes far more wrinkle-free than a plain old carrier bag. Those made by Eagle Creek come highly recommended and are sold all over the place: www.eaglecreek.com/accessories/packing_folders. You could also experiment with using an ordinary suit carrier and attaching it to your back rack with bungee cords. Those who refuse to invest in a specific suit-carrying pannier swear by rolling, rather than folding.

Another option would be to go for a bespoke cycling suit, such as those made by Dashing Tweeds (www.dashingtweeds.co.uk). These are made with a clever fabric which appears normal by day but reflective by night. But they do not come cheap – the undoubtedly beautiful ladies' 'Lumatwill' cape was being sold for £400 at the time of writing.

I must admit, however, that the smartest bike commuters I know do not transport their suits by bike but keep them in the office to slip into on arrival.

I'M NOT FIT ENOUGH

I doubt this very much. The joy of cycling is that, unlike running, almost anyone can do it. If you are really heavy, there are special bikes designed to take extra weight, but for the vast majority of people, any old machine will do. Sure, you'll find it hard work at first if you're desperately out of shape – and do expect to get sweaty – but you'll be astonished how quickly your fitness improves. Alan Sugar lost three stone when he swapped his limo for a bicycle.

Pedalling means prizes

In Germany, health insurers have caught on to the fact that cyclists have fewer health problems. Since 2001, the biggest health insurance firm, AOK, has sponsored a scheme called Mit Dem Rad Zur Arbeit (Go to Work by Bike), which rewards customers who cycle to work with the chance to win prizes. The programme takes place for three months over the summer, and anyone who commutes for at least twenty days in that period is eligible to win cruises, dream holidays and electric bikes. In 2008, 168,000 people took part.

I'M SO BAD AT MORNINGS, I CAN'T EVEN CONTEMPLATE FOOD, LET ALONE GET ON A BIKE

Cycling is far better at waking you up than being squished on a stuffy bus. Splash some cold water on your face before you leave the house and saddle up. You'll be wide awake by the time you get to the end of your road.

I LIVE TOO FAR AWAY

Everybody has their own idea about what constitutes too far, but I think that any bicycle commute that takes more than an hour each way is pushing it a bit. Twenty minutes to half an hour is ideal, I reckon. Less than twenty minutes, and you'll spend almost as long each end locking and unlocking it; more than thirty and you really will need a shower.

If you have further to go, you could investigate hybrid options, such as taking your bike on a train or bus part of the way. Geeks call this 'mixed-mode commuting'. If you're travelling at peak times, you may well, however, only be allowed on public transport with a folding bike. For more information on folding bikes, see chapter 1. For tips on negotiating public transport with a bike, see p.211.

I HAVE TOO MUCH TO CARRY

In countries such as India and China, where bicycling is a perfectly normal way to transport people and goods about, nothing is deemed too big, bulky or ridiculous to take from A to B using pedal power. You must at some point have seen a photo of a tiny sparrow of a man perched on a bicycle somehow trailing hundreds of coconuts/a mysterious amount of polystyrene/enough furniture to kit out a townhouse. When I was growing up, our window cleaner used to cycle around with his ladder and bucket and, pedalling around town, I've seen cyclists transporting everything from a coffee table to a small dinghy. I once saw a man in north London nonchalantly carrying two kitchen sinks by bike.

However, if you have a lot of stuff to schlep about – you're a teacher with thirty exercise books to lug home and mark, for example – you will need a bike capable of fitting a luggage rack on the front or back (see chapters 1 and 2). Many bikes have the bosses (little holes) in the frame into which you screw the rack.

You can buy really big panniers these days, and there is also the option of securing odd shaped items to a rack with a bungee cord. Sometimes I have two full panniers and a big cake tin strapped to the back of my bike, as well as a handbag across my chest, and end up transporting far more than I would ever have been able to carry on the bus. See p.75 for more info about panniers.

I HAVE TO CARRY A LAPTOP

OK. This is easily do-able. There are loads of different options here, from simply cycling with your usual laptop bag slung on your back, to tailor-made panniers. Be very careful with panniers, though, as they need to be very well padded to protect your machine from the vibrations caused by bumps in the road. Generally, the more you pay, the better the protection. Arkel's 'Commuter' pannier comes recommended, but it costs well over £100.

Assuming your laptop isn't from the dark ages and is relatively light, a messenger style shoulder bag is probably your best bet. For extra protection, you can wrap the computer in a padded sleeve, probably made out of a wetsuity sort of material, which will also help keep it dry.

You could also investigate a hardshell backpack, which has a plastic casing designed to protect your computer should you fall off. Be warned: with this extra protection comes added weight, and there's something a little Red Dwarf about the look. Makes to look out for include Carradice (www.carradice.co.uk) and Arkel (www.arkel-od.com), as well as Ortlieb (www.ortlieb.de).

To be extra safe, always shut your laptop down properly before you transport it anywhere by bike. A sudden jolt can cause the computer accidentally to latch open, and it can start to fire up. Far more damage will be caused to the hard drive if it's in use when you hit a nasty pothole.

THERE'S NOWHERE SAFE TO LOCK IT AT WORK

If there is no secure bike shed or storage facility on site, and you don't feel happy about locking up your pride and joy on the street, it is worth asking your boss whether you can bring your bike inside. If they say no, point out that many local authorities provide grants to encourage employers to install cycle parking. These grants sometimes also offer matching funding for changing facilities, showers and lockers.

Bike parking doesn't have to take up nearly as much space as they might imagine, as bikes can be stored vertically, or even stacked on top of each other like bunk beds. Point out that they can fit in at least five bikes in the space one car takes up, possibly twice that if they're clever. I've seen forty-two folded Bromptons squeezed into one parking space.

Cycling advocacy organizations such as the CTC can sometimes arrange free cycle audits for firms, to advise on how to best use the available space. Transport for London suggests providing parking for everyone who already pedals to work, plus another 50 per cent, followed by another 20 per cent every time bike stand occupancy levels reach 80 per cent. Good luck with that.

CTC and Sustrans have produced a handy guide to good cycle parking. Download the PDF here and leave it on your boss's desk: www.ctc.org.uk/resources/campaigns/cycleparkinfo.pdf

I GO OUT MOST NIGHTS STRAIGHT FROM WORK

Take your bike with you. It's a good deterrent from drinking too much on a school night. If you don't want to hold back on the booze front, leave your bike at the office. You can just pick it up the next day, or whenever you opt to have a night in.

The firm where cycling = days off

Forster, a London-based PR company, rewards employees who walk or cycle to work with extra time off. For every journey to and from work that is made by foot or bike, employees earn five minutes' holiday, which can add up to a total of two and a half extra days a year.

I'M WORRIED
ABOUT THE POLLUTION

It's understandable – every time I find myself in heavy traffic, I do question whether the workout my lungs are getting is cancelled out by the fumes I'm breathing in. But research has shown that car users inhale more harmful gases sitting in their vehicles than cyclists travelling among them. That said, there is no denying that it is deeply unpleasant copping a mouth full of exhaust fumes when caught behind a bus or juggernaut. Wherever possible, avoid major roads, particularly during rush hour.

DO I NEED ONE OF THOSE
SARS-STYLE FACE MASKS?

I doubt it. No one has proved conclusively that they work, they get unpleasantly sweaty and you'll look like a paranoid conspiracy theorist. The reason they don't seem to do what they're supposed to do is that the harmful carbon particles are so tiny that no type of expensive mask and filter can block them.

WHAT IF I GET A PUNCTURE?

You'll cope. If you're not going far and you've got a slow puncture, you might just about get away with cycling it gently to your destination. At my office, the cyclists all chipped in a pound until we had enough to buy a track pump to keep in the carpark for emergencies.

In an ideal world, you'll have a pump, tyre levers and a spare inner tube with you and you can fix it yourself (see chapter 4). Before I learned how to mend my own bike, I found that standing by the side of the road looking upset/puzzled tended to attract the attention/sympathy of passing cyclists, and some white knight would always answer my distress call.

In big cities, there are firms or one-man-bands you can call up to come and fix your bike, rather like the AA. Google 'mobile bicycle repair' to find your nearest service.

You can also buy insurance that provides cyclists with similar breakdown assistance to that enjoyed by motorists. Breakdown cover ensures that if you are unable to complete your journey as a result of an accident, vandalism or irreparable breakdown (excluding punctures), then you and your bike will be taken to a railway station, bike shop, home or work. You do have to question whether it's really worth losing your no-claims bonus for this, however.

CTC, the main national cyclists' organization, offers this sort of cover for £52 per year (see www.ctc.org.uk) and ETA, the Environmental Transport Association, offers Cycle Rescue cover from £34 per year (www.eta.co.uk/breakdown/cycle_rescue).

To minimize your chances of getting a puncture, you could put puncture-resistant tyres on your bike. These are not as slick as your standard road tyre, but unless you're racing or travelling long distances, you shouldn't notice too much of a difference. For more on puncture avoidance, see p.122.

I'LL BE TOO TIRED WHEN I ARRIVE

If you're cycling a silly distance, this may be true. But I actually find that my twenty-minute bicycling blast wakes me up in the morning, and I arrive at my desk far more alert than I would be if I had come in on a stuffy bus. I'm also far less grumpy than I would be had I spent the morning banging my fists on the steering wheel as I went nowhere fast.

I'LL GET A SORE BUM

Sore bottom syndrome (SBS) is pretty unavoidable when you first start cycling. That bit of your body isn't used to taking your weight in quite that way, and you'll inevitably feel it when you get out of the saddle, and the following day. But after a week or so of daily cycling, you'll have worn in your saddle – and bottom – and the pain will go away. Promise. Until you start cycling long distances, that is, then you'll graduate from SBS to full-on saddle sores. I'll spare you the gory details on these beauties until chapter 9 (cycling for sport).

There are, however, ways to alleviate SBS. First of all, adjust your existing saddle (up, down, forward, back) to see if that makes any difference. If that doesn't work, buy a different one. Don't always assume the bigger and springier the better, though a friend of mine swapped her hard racing saddle for something she lovingly refers to as the 'mattress' and has never looked back. Many people swear by an old-fashioned leather saddle made by Brooks (www.brooksengland.com), though they do take quite a while to break in. You might also consider installing a shock-absorbing seat post.

You could also invest in a pair of the dreaded padded cycling shorts. Completely hideous but, my, you'll feel the benefit.

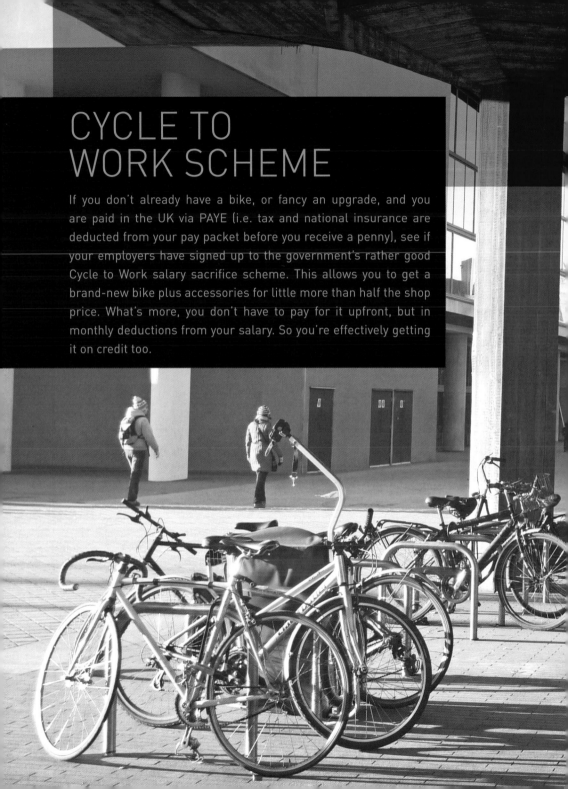

CYCLE TO WORK SCHEME

If you don't already have a bike, or fancy an upgrade, and you are paid in the UK via PAYE (i.e. tax and national insurance are deducted from your pay packet before you receive a penny), see if your employers have signed up to the government's rather good Cycle to Work salary sacrifice scheme. This allows you to get a brand-new bike plus accessories for little more than half the shop price. What's more, you don't have to pay for it upfront, but in monthly deductions from your salary. So you're effectively getting it on credit too.

Your employer gives you a voucher to buy the bike of your choice plus whatever bits and bobs you need to go with it (helmets, lights, locks, etc). Most bike shops are signed up to some version of the scheme or other, so you shouldn't have problems finding one to take your voucher. Generally, there's a £1,000 limit on the whole package but, ultimately, it's up to your employer.

For the duration of the scheme – usually eighteen months – your employer notionally owns the bike, and 'loans' it to you in equal monthly instalments as a tax-free benefit. You pay no income tax, national insurance or VAT on the repayments, which can equal a saving of up to 50 per cent off the recommended retail price, depending on your tax bracket. Even if you're a low earner, you'll still get at least a 35 per cent discount.

At the end of the period, the bike still officially belongs to your employers, and they are supposed to 'sell' it back to you for a fair fee, unlikely to be more than 5 per cent of the original price. But, in practice, they'll probably not bother and the bike will be yours for ever. Hurrah.

Bear in mind that if the bike is stolen or damaged, you'll still have to pay the monthly instalments, so insurance is advisable. And if you're made redundant or otherwise leave the company with which you started the salary sacrifice scheme, you'll need to repay the outstanding amount with your final pay cheque. You have to sign something saying you'll only use the bike to cycle to work too, though of course this no longer applies after you leave the firm or have paid back the loan.

There are a growing number of third party organizations that have signed up to help people take advantage of the Cycle to Work scheme. You'll have to go with whichever one your employer has linked up with. Some are not linked to a particular chain of bike shops but provide vouchers which can be used at a wide range of selected outlets. Examples include:

- ↘ **www.cyclescheme.co.uk**
- ↘ **www.cyclesolutions.co.uk**
- ↘ **www.onyourbike.gb.com**
- ↘ **www.cycletoworknow.com**

OTHER TAX BREAKS

If you are self-employed, you can claim back 20 pence per mile for all work-related bike journeys – note that this does not cover cycling to and from your work, but journeys taken as part of your work.

POOL BIKE SCHEMES

Some enlightened employers have set up pool bike schemes, which provide a number of bicycles and safety equipment for the use of the workforce. These bikes are maintained by the company and can be offered to employees for any kind of journey, but are typically used for work-related trips, such as local meetings, travel between sites and visiting clients.

A pilot scheme in the London Borough of Southwark gave organizations, including the Tate Modern, the chance to trial a bike pool of between one and five bikes. At the end of the six months, the bikes could be kept on a hire basis, or bought by the firm or individual employees.

Of the twenty-four organizations involved, over half paid to keep some of their pool bikes at the end of the free trial. At the start of the scheme, 8 per cent of those surveyed cycled for work-related journeys at least once a week. By the end of the scheme, this had risen to 21 per cent. Over the same period, the number of people who drove to work decreased from 11 per cent to 6 per cent.

Get paid to commute

In some areas of Birmingham, Alabama, commuters are paid to forgo their cars and cycle to work. GetGreen offers commuters $2 (£1.20) per day, up to $120 (£73) over a three-month period, to anyone who lives or works in Jefferson or Shelby counties, when they change their commutes from driving alone to carpool, take public transport, bike or walk to work.

www.commutesmarter.org

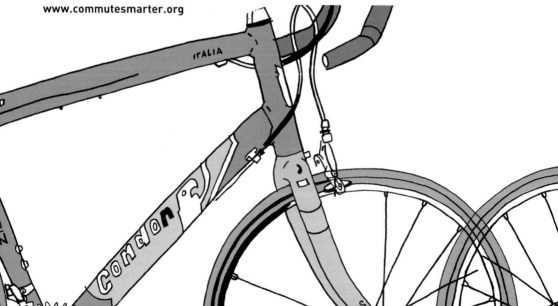

Many TV news anchors these days have a reputation for being high maintenance sissies who spend more time in Make-up than out on the mean streets. Not Channel 4's Jon Snow, who scoots around London on his Condor hybrid, pedalling furiously from Whitehall to press conferences and back to the studio.

Snow, president of the CTC since 2007, is the perfect example of a man who fits cycling into his life rather than the other way around – 'a jobbing cyclist' is how he describes himself. He wears a suit while cycling, with trouser clips to protect the fabric from the oily chain.

He keeps a punchy blog at http://blogs.channel4.com/snowblog, which often talks about his two-wheeled adventures. A typical post might see him bemoaning the theft of his beloved machine or ranting about the poor bike parking facilities at Parliament – he learned the hard way that Westminster police blow up bikes locked to railings, or smash the lock and cart the machine off to the cells. 'The very fact that the seat of government remains so actively hostile to bikes ("We're concerned about bicycle bombs, old chap") speaks volumes about our real attitudes to green technology,' wrote Snow. 'What chance reversing climate change if you can't park your bloody bike anywhere near the seat of the government charged with trying to fix it?'

CYCLING FOR LEISURE

t is a waste of a bicycle to only ride it to work. You could pedal on for a picnic, spend a long weekend exploring a new area or even embark on a full-on cycling holiday. You can either do it all under your own steam, carrying with you everything you need (this is occasionally known as 'bike-packing', a phrase so lumpen I promise never to use it again), or bribe a friend with a car to be your support vehicle and meet you at the other end. There are lots of specialist bike-tour companies who can plan an itinerary for you if you feel daunted going it alone or want to enjoy a holiday with like-minded strangers.

You don't have to cycle all the way – with a little planning you can combine rides with train journeys, car trips and flights. Especially if you live in the middle of a big city, there is no shame in jumping on a train to skip the grotty suburbs. Getting from the centre of London to the countryside involves 15 miles of soot and traffic lights, which I prefer to miss out with a half-hour train journey. Mind you, nothing beats the Wonder Woman feeling of empowerment after completing a trip by pedal power alone.

Some of my most magical holidays have involved a bit – or a lot – of cycling. I once spent a fortnight cycling from my house in east London all the way to Land's End, and I've often biked over the Downs to Brighton for the day at the beach. Recently, my boyfriend and I took our bikes to the Alps and tortured ourselves on some Tour de France climbs. A friend and I once booked to see King Lear at Stratford-upon-Avon and cycled part of the way home, and when we went to Barcelona we hired bikes to explore the city. I've larked around Paris on a rented Vélib' one midsummer's eve and I did the Dunwich Dynamo, an exhilarating (if knackering) 120-mile overnight ride from Hackney to the Suffolk coast, with hundreds of others.

Cycling is by far and away the best way to see the countryside. It's far less tedious than walking, and pootling along at 10mph you absorb all sorts of sights, smells and sounds that you'd miss in the car or on the train: the tonk of a cricket ball as you near a village green, a swan's nest by a rural pond, a river just made for a dip on a hot sunny day. My Land's End trip took me from the traffic-clogged streets of the capital, along the Thames past Windsor Castle, into the rolling hills of Wiltshire, accidentally across a live firing range on Salisbury Plain, into Somerset, up the horrifically steep hill out of Minehead and down into Exmoor, along the Tarka Trail in Devon, down to the stunning beach at Crackington Haven in Cornwall and finally to the anticlimactic tourist trap that is Land's End.

On all of my adventures, my best bit has been lunch. Even the simplest pub ploughman's salad tastes like heaven after a bike ride. Never underestimate how hungry cycling can make you – always have a flapjack or energy bar stashed away somewhere in case you start flagging. Or, better still, schedule in a tea-room stop along the way. When I finish this book, have promised to take my best friend to the Fat Duck restaurant in Bray – if she'll cycle there with me.

If you're not used to cycling long distances, don't go mad the first time you decide to go for a bike ride. Even a flat route of 10 miles can be a lot for a relatively fit newcomer; add in a few hills and you'll be truly exhausted. When I first started cycling for fun, my companion and I got the train to Ely in Cambridgeshire and cycled the 16-mile pancake-flat route to Cambridge. When we arrived, I thought I'd never walk again. Now I can do 40 miles on the level almost without noticing.

Your options are limitless if you have a bike that can go off-road. You could explore your local forest or tackle the Himalayas or the Andes, follow the Great Wall of China, explore the Amazon basin, cross deserts. Providing you are careful not to disturb the local flora and fauna and are sure of getting enough food and drink, you can go more or less where you like.

If you want something more structured for a day trip, you could try out a mountain-bike trail: those in Wales and Scotland are considered some of the world's finest, but the UK is full of forests and converted quarries to explore. At home and abroad, ski resorts turn into downhill mountain-bike Meccas in the summer months, and the ski lifts even keep running so you don't have to sweat on the ascent. There is fantastic mountain biking in Canada, and in California and Colorado in the States, as well as in Austria, Switzerland and New Zealand.

For information on tackling a charity bike ride, see the next chapter.

CYCLE TOURING

Touring is the rather old-fashioned name for using your bike to explore new places – a way of getting somewhere while enjoying yourself along the way. Talking of 'touring' always sounds rather grand to me, as if tourers fancy themselves as characters in *A Room With a View*. You can do a day tour, where you return to base in the evening, or a longer tour over days, weeks, months or even years. Cycle touring can be combined with other hobbies – wine enthusiasts can plot a route from vineyard to vineyard in rural France, wild swimmers can seek out hidden lakes and riverbanks, keen photographers can take advantage of the fact that a bicycle, unlike a car, doesn't scare off wild animals.

You can build a tour around anything you fancy. I once read about some curious fleas kept in a cabinet in the Natural History Museum in Tring, Hertfordshire. In the article, an actress being interviewed about her favourite museum claimed these fleas were dressed as Mexicans. One was apparently wearing a sombrero; the other was cooking a tortilla. I couldn't believe it. So it was that I ended up cycling from my house to the museum, with an overnight stop in a B&B on a farm in the lovely village of Dinton to see whether this could possibly be true. We made it to Tring on the second day, locked our bikes up outside the museum and raced straight upstairs to the insect section to peer through a microscope to see what did indeed appear to be real (albeit dead) fleas in Mexican fancy dress. No one believes me, but it's true.

One day, I'd love to cycle the length of the former border between East and West Germany, stopping at Cold War sights along the way. Scholars of the First World War could do a battlefield tour in northern France and Belgium. If you love cheese, you could go from Wensleydale to Caerphilly via Gloucester and Shropshire.

The best way to ease yourself into cycle touring is simply to pick a nice-looking spot 5 miles or so from your house, then cycle there and back or, better, work out a circular route. That way you'll be able to gauge whether your bike is comfortable for longer distances, if you have the right gear and whether your legs can take it. It won't cost you a penny, and you may be surprised what you find en route. I did this when I moved to Hackney in east London and stumbled upon all manner of things I'd never have discovered otherwise - such as a huge urban blackberry patch, a kayak-hire shop, a riding school, the favoured picnicking spot of all the Orthodox Jews living in nearby Stamford Hill and a canal-side café serving marvellous cakes.

If you're planning a multi-day tour and are relatively new to the saddle, plan to gradually build up your mileage. The advice tends to be for each day to be not more than two-thirds of the distance you could do in a one-off ride.

WHAT BIKE?

You don't need a specific 'touring bike' to go cycle touring, but you may need to make a few adjustments to your existing ride – fitting fatter, knobbly tyres if you're planning any off-roading, for example. Proper touring bikes look like road bikes but with slightly longer and sturdier frames, usually made out of steel, which are designed to carry luggage and withstand harsh knocks. If you are going up hills, especially with a well-laden machine, make sure you have a range of low gears, otherwise you'll soon find yourself pushing. Don't assume that because you have a folding bike you can't attempt a tour – some models are designed to be ridden longer distances.

CLOTHES

You don't necessarily need any special kit for long rides, though this might be the moment to invest in some sort of padded bottoms if you haven't already. Wearing padded cycling shorts or trousers (they don't have to be tight and Lycra) really can be the difference between a pain-free backside and one riddled with saddle sores. You can always disguise the shorts if you find them offensive. I got to the top of the Col du Grand St Bernard on the Swiss/Italian border (altitude 2,473m) in a rather nice dress with padded pedal-pushers underneath.

This is also the time to conquer clipless pedals, if you haven't already (see p. 66). When you're not having to stop for traffic lights every thirty seconds, you'll really feel the benefit of having your feet clamped to the pedals, especially when going uphill. And it's always worth taking a lightweight waterproof. The thinnest ones scrunch up small enough to fit in the back pocket of a cycling jersey or into a saddlebag. I'd highly recommend gloves, too. You'll be surprised how much unprotected palms can ache after a long day cycling, and you'll be glad of the protection if you fall off too.

If you're doing a multi-day tour, take at least one spare set of clothes to wear at night so that you don't put everyone else off their tea when you walk into the pub. I usually go for a lightweight pair of trousers, some flip-flops, a vest and a jumper. Hardly high fashion, but I'm usually too zonked to care.

BOTTLE CAGES

Definitely fit one or two bottle cages to your bike. If you look on your frame, you should have a number of bosses (little holes) where the cages attach. The cages are very cheap and easy to install and are the best way of carrying liquid on the go. Much easier than faffing around with ridiculous-looking Camelbacks, those rucksacks which drip-feed you through a tube like a coma patient.

LUGGAGE

Unless you are travelling really light or have persuaded some sucker to take your clobber to your destination, you'll need a way of carrying stuff that doesn't involve you wearing a rucksack – probably panniers attached to a rack. If your bike doesn't have mounting points to fit a standard rack, you could install a seatpost-mounted rack. If you're schlepping a lot of gear, you could use a trailer, but it will slow you down something rotten. Whatever you go for, try to distribute the weight evenly; if you put too much on the back, you'll have a job steering.

The best advice I can give you is to take as little as possible. Lumbering along with heavy, bulging panniers can make a light bike handle like a tractor. A saddlebag is always a good idea, as you can dip into it as you go along.

If you're hardy enough to go cycle camping, it is worth investing in the lightest, most compact kit you can get your hands on, otherwise you'll find yourself laden down like an overburdened packhorse. Shop around, and you can find a tent weighing less than 1.5kg (3.3lb), though you'll likely pay a pretty penny for it. These tents often divide conveniently into two, so the weight can be shared between cyclists. Then you'll need a sleeping bag, maybe a carry-mat, a stove, a pot, eating and drinking utensils, and so on.

On the opposite end of the scale is 'credit-card touring', where you take little more than a change of clothes and plastic money. But even staying in B&Bs or hostels, the costs still mount up.

See chapter 2 for a detailed discussion on carrying stuff by bike.

LOCK

Depending on where you will stop en route, you may still need to take one of these, I'm afraid, though it needn't be as heavy as the one you'd use for commuting. If you're going somewhere remote and civilized, such as the Isle of Skye, you will obviously not need nearly as tough a lock as if you were doing an urban tour through a big city.

TOOLS

If you're embarking on a bit of a trek, make sure you at least know how to change a flat tyre (see chapter 4). But you could well cycle for hundreds, if not thousands, of miles without anything going wrong. When James Bowthorpe broke the world record for cycling around the world in 2009, he didn't get one puncture from Hyde Park in London all the way to the middle of Australia, despite an attempted kidnapping in Iran and a serious illness that forced a five-day rest stop in Bangkok. 'After that I got several in quick succession in the back tyre, which were just as frustrating to fix in the middle of the Nullarbor [an arid plain in Australia] as they are in Balham,' he told the *Guardian*.

ROUTE PLANNING

Despite the march of technology, I still rely on old-fashioned Ordnance Survey (OS) maps to plan bike rides in the UK. I get the pink Landranger ones with the 1:50,000 scale – they are detailed enough to show the quietest roads but also cover a lot of ground (an area of 40km by 40km/25 miles by 25 miles). They show virtually every path, track and road, as well as very important features such as pubs. Be careful if you decide to follow footpaths, unless you particularly enjoy hauling your bicycle over stiles and through kissing gates. While following a bridleway once, my companion and I also learned that cows don't like bikes at all. New OS maps show the path of the wonderful National Cycle Network, which you can also view online here: www.nationalcyclenetwork.org.uk

The downside of maps is that they take up space. When we went to Land's End we had to carry ten maps to cover the 500-mile route, though I know some people on long trips simply post maps back home once they're obsolete. They are also almost impossible to read on the go, even if you have a handlebar-mounted map reader like the type rookie London cabbies use when learning the Knowledge by scooter.

For day trips, especially in winter if I don't want to be stopping too often to check the map, I just plan a route and write a list of all the villages I need to go through, which I keep in my back pocket to check. If you can't be bothered messing around folding maps, you could always tear out a page from a road atlas, though this is not a very sustainable habit.

If you're looking for ideas for day trips in the UK, the environmental charity Sustrans has some great suggestions listed on www.sustrans. org.uk – just look for 'easy rides' listed under the region you're interested in. Most local tourist boards also have information on nice bike rides in their areas. The CTC has a library of over 700 route maps covering all over the world, though you have to be a member to access them.

If you are frightened of hills, make sure you know how to read map contours – which, for those who need a geography refresher course, are the wiggly lines which link all the points which are at the same height above sea level. The closer the contour lines are together, the steeper the slope, and vice versa. Remember: the shortest route between two points is often the steepest.

Beware of any roads with little arrowheads on them – they indicate steep climbs. One arrow means a gradient of 14–20 per cent; two together signal a terrifying 20 per cent or steeper, which means for every five metres you travel along, you climb at least one metre. This hurts. I have been known to take ridiculously long detours to avoid a category-two hill after an agonizing experience on Porlock Hill in Minehead, Somerset. Thought to be the UK's steepest A-road, it has a 25 per cent gradient in places and a seemingly endless number of hairpin bends. There were tears.

If, when route planning, you want to estimate how far you'll be going, you can use a small map measure, a little metal roller device which you run along your proposed route to measure the distance in either miles or kilometres. You can also go for the more old-school method of using a bit of string. New-schoolers rely on the internet, perhaps plotting their route on www.gmap-pedometer.com, though this isn't so good if you're straying away from roads. Unless you're somewhere really remote, it's often a good idea to stay within ten miles or so of a train station in case you get tired and want to go home.

If you want some inspiration for planning a new route, there are lots of websites where cyclists can share their favourite rides, usually plotted using Google Maps. A lot of people like www.bikely.com too.

GPS

Gadget fiends prefer to navigate via GPS (global positioning system), either using a standalone device or their phone. The big problem with this is that they tend to run out of battery quite quickly, so unless you are sure you will be near a plug point every evening, forget it. That said, at the time of writing, bike manufacturer Dahon was about to launch an add-on which charges a phone battery as you pedal, as well as a handlebar mount especially for iPhones.

I have a fancy Garmin GPS system, which can do all sorts of wizardry, but I think it's better for training than navigation. It isn't very good at choosing pleasant routes and has a tendency to send me off down horrible A-roads unless I laboriously key in my own journey. And, anyway, I like maps. You spot all sorts of things on them, from Roman ruins to stone circles, which GPS isn't nearly subtle enough to pick up.

Navigation-wise, what GPS is good for, however, is sharing routes with other people. If you've done a great ride and are feeling all evangelical about it, you can upload your route to various websites (such as www.mapmyride.com), where others will also be happy to share their own tips. If you have a GPS-enabled Nokia phone, you can download the Sports Tracker programme which stores all your rides and tells you your speed and distance (http://sportstracker.nokia.com).

TRAINS, PLANES, FERRIES AND AUTOMOBILES

TRAINS

The intractable bike policies on most UK trains make me howl. Despite the government's pledge to encourage cycling, it has yet to get the hang of joined-up transport planning and train companies are not really obliged to do anything special to accommodate cyclists onboard. Some appear to go out of their way to make it difficult. Always check before you travel, and do reserve a bike place if they are available.

On some services, space for bikes is severely limited – the huge Pendolino trains on Virgin's west-coast line only take four bikes in total, and Northern trains accept a paltry two, for example. Virgin, in particular, tends to make an enormous fuss if you rock up without a specific bike reservation, even if there is space. Other companies are more relaxed, and let you hop on with a bike at any carriage, though you might have to guard it by the door, in case the doors open at the wrong side. Some trains have special bike carriages, but you'll need ESP to work out where that might be before the train arrives, so prepare yourself for a mad dash up the other end of the platform. And steel yourself for a major battle if you're in a group of cyclists.

Forget trying to take any unfolding bicycles on any commuter trains to or from London during rush hour, which for trains going into the capital means any arriving between 7 and 10 a.m., or leaving London between 4 and 7 p.m.

For an outline of the different bike policies on UK trains, see www.nationalrail.co.uk/passenger_services/cyclists.html

Brompton has also produced a handy fact sheet outlining the bike policies on all UK trains, which you can download from the National Rail site.

Other countries take a far more enlightened approach. You'll have no problem in the Scandinavian countries or Germany, and you can take a bike on the Eurostar to France or Belgium with a £20 reservation (space permitting). The best site for researching trains and bikes in Europe is the English version of the German Rail site, www.bahn.de – just click on the English option. It doesn't just cover Germany.

The Bike Access website provides a good overview of travelling with bikes on trains and planes all over the world: www.bikeaccess.net

PLANES

This requires planning. You usually need to warn the airline in advance that you are bringing a bike (some will levy a surcharge for this), and you'll often have to take it to bits and put it in a bike bag or box. You can either buy these to use again, or if you're nice to your local bike shop they might give you a cardboard one for free. Whichever you choose, they are all too bulky to carry by bike, so you'll not be able to cycle to the airport. The CTC sells cheap, transparent, heavy-duty poly bags – some people swear by these, as they believe it encourages airport staff to take a little more care when there is no ambiguity what they are dealing with. Hardshell bike cases are probably your safest option, but they make a convenient base for slinging other luggage on top and disguise the precious contents within.

Some airlines allow bikes to be checked in intact. According to the CTC, when bikes fly naked, they paradoxically seem to suffer no more damage than when they go covered – usually less, perhaps because airport staff know exactly what they are dealing with. But if you do have to dismantle your bike, at the very least you'll have to turn the handlebars sideways and take the pedals off. It is a myth that you need to deflate the tyres for safety reasons (they won't pop as cargo holds are pressurized), but many airline staff don't know any better and insist you let the air out before they'll accept the bike for travel. If you can, leave a little air in, though, as it is better protection for your wheels. It's worth swaddling the bike in bubble wrap and putting a big 'fragile' sticker on the outside of the box, as baggage handlers aren't known for their sensitivity. Check in advance that there is somewhere at the destination airport where you can store your empty bag or box, otherwise you'll have to buy disposable boxes at both ends. Beware if you decide to take your lock and pedal spanner as hand luggage. Bird-brained security people may take some convincing that you will not try to hijack the plane with such dangerous weapons.

If you're checking your bike into the hold, make sure in advance that it doesn't go over the weight limit. On cheap flights especially, anything over 15kg incurs a heavy excess-baggage supplement – and if you're checking in panniers as well as a bike, it's quite easy to go over the limit.

The CTC website has a comprehensive guide to taking bikes on planes: www.ctc.org.uk

FERRIES

It is usually quite simple to take bikes on ferries – even those which only take foot passengers. The exception tends to be commuter ferries, which often ban all but folding bikes, especially during peak times. Sometimes you need to make a special reservation and pay a small supplement, but it's generally free. Always check in advance that you'll be allowed on. If it's a car ferry, bikes are normally asked to check-in with motorised vehicles rather than with foot passengers, and you then shackle your bike to the side of the boat using ropes provided. The big advantage over flying is that you don't have to dismantle the bike, or let air out of the tyres, and can roll straight off the ferry and start your holiday.

There is a more detailed guide here: www.cycletourer.co.uk/cycletouring/ferries.shtm

ALTERNATIVELY. . .

If you're only trying to get from the UK to mainland Europe, the European Bike Express (www.bike-express.co.uk) is an alternative to flying, and offers a coach service with purpose-built bike trailers from numerous English towns to destinations across France, including the Mediterranean and Atlantic coasts.

BIKE RACKS FOR CARS

If you want to take bikes in a car, you have a number of options. If you don't have any passengers in the rear and not too much luggage, you might be able to put the back seats down and fit in a bike or two quite easily, as long as you take the front wheel(s) off. I used to do this in a VW Polo with no major problems. If you do this, always put the bikes in with the delicate rear mech (i.e. the oily cogs) facing upwards.

You could also buy a bike rack for either your car roof or boot. There are three main kinds of racks but, whichever you choose, remember to lock the bikes to the rack if you're stopping somewhere public.

TOWBAR AND TOWBALL-MOUNTED RACKS

If you have a towbar or ball, use it. That way, the rack won't even touch the car and the whole set-up is really secure. These racks typically hold up to four bikes and, because they keep the bikes relatively low, you won't feel them dragging you down quite so much as with many strap-on racks. You may have the same lights/number plate-obstruction problem as with strap-mounted racks, however.

STRAP-MOUNTED RACKS

These hook on to your boot and are cheap and simple to use on cars without towbars or roof rails, though there's an art to fixing them on securely enough. The downer is that you can't open the boot while it's attached, and you have to be really careful not to scratch the car's paintwork or obscure your rear lights or number plate. If they do hide your lights or number plate, you'll have to buy a plates-and-lights kit and attach it to your bikes.

ROOF RACKS

If your car has roof bars, you can fit a roof rack to carry two to four bikes. They're generally quite secure – just don't forget they're on when you go under a low barrier at a car park.

CLASSIC BIKE RIDES

THE END-TO-END

The big adventure most UK road cyclists would like to tick off at some point in their life is pedalling from the southernmost point of Britain to the most northerly – cycling from Land's End to John O'Groat's (or the other way around, though most go south to north as there tend to be more helpful winds). There are whole books and websites dedicated to End-to-Ending, but you can make it as easy or as difficult as you like. If you have someone who loves you enough, you could get them to drive with you and carry your stuff. For a hefty fee (usually £1,500 upwards) you could join a supported tour through a travel company. Even the most direct route for a car is 837 miles, but unless you want to spend a lot of time on busy A roads, you're likely to end up doing at least 1,000 miles. Most cyclists take at least ten days to cover this distance, though there are lunatics who have done it in less than forty-eight hours. If you look on the internet, there are dozens of different route suggestions, including a few that stay completely off-road and others which aim to visit as many real ale pubs as possible.

THE COAST-TO-COAST

A gentler option is to traverse the UK from east to west or vice versa. The classic routes run from Whitehaven or Workington on the Cumbrian coast to Sunderland or Tynemouth on the North Sea coast. Most people take three or four days, following the National Cycle Network's very visible CTC signs:
www.c2c-guide.co.uk

COASTS AND CASTLES

This 200-mile journey follows Route 1 of the National Cycle Network and takes in some of Britain's best bits, including Hadrian's Wall, miles of unspoilt coastline, the beautiful Tweed Valley and, finally, Edinburgh: **www.nationalcyclenetwork.org.uk**

CORK TO KERRY

Despite its legendarily shoddy roads, Ireland has long been a favourite destination for bicycle tourists. Pedalling around the south-west of the country is a great way to experience the stunning landscape.

LONDON TO BRIGHTON

Probably the most famous route out of London, this 60-mile ride is pretty easy going – until you hit Ditchling Beacon in the South Downs and start sweating. If you want to miss out the trafficky start, get a train to Box Hill or even Haywards Heath and pedal on from there.

MOUNTAIN BIKING

You can do a tour on a mountain bike, of course, but a knobbly-tyred beast will really come into its own when you take it off-piste and into the wild. If your machine has suspension, all the better.

Though it still has the image of a hardcore sport practised by reckless young men who like throwing themselves down hills, mountain biking is a good activity for families. It's away from traffic, you can make it as hard or as easy as you like and, if you fall off, you'll hit ground rather softer than tarmac (which can still hurt, of course, so you might want to wear some protective gear).

To ease yourself into mountain biking, simply get out in the countryside and have a go. Bicycles can legally use bridleways, so start off on them to get the hang of riding over rough ground.

You could also look for a trail centre in a region you fancy visiting. These are specialist centres with graded trails, jump parks and top-notch facilities to suit all ages and abilities, and will almost always hire you a bike if you don't have one. Often the trails are colour-coded in order of difficulty, like ski slopes, and generally include downhill courses as well as cross-country trails.

There are three main kinds of mountain biking – cross country (XC), downhill (DH) and free riding. Beginners generally start with XC, as it takes place at much slower speeds (and lower altitudes) than the others, and the mixture of down- and uphills on muddy and rocky ground makes it a good way to practise handling a mountain bike.

If you're going to try downhill biking, you'll need body armour and nerves of steel. Ditto free riding, which essentially involves doing whatever you like – but often entails jumping off high ledges and ridges.

In Britain, the Forestry Commission looks after mountain-bike trails in over 205 forests, which amounts to over 2,600km of way-marked cycle trails. Search on the Commission's website by the name of the forest or nearest town, or search by the country or county: www.forestry.gov.uk

In Northern Ireland, the scene is less developed, but Gortin Glen Forest Park near Omagh in County Tyrone is officially appointed for the use of mountain biking: www.forestserviceni.gov.uk

CYCLING HOLIDAYS

If you want to embark on a cycling holiday without the hassle of organizing it yourself, why not book a guided tour via a specialized travel company? These firms offer trips all over the world and cater for all ages, abilities and price ranges. There are a number of advantages in doing it this way, the main one being that someone else will transport your luggage. You also have the benefit of experienced guides, who will scope out the best routes, stopping points and accommodation. The downer is that they are often awfully expensive, and unless you book a very costly private guide, you'll be spending day after day with strangers who may or may not become your new best friends. Some tour companies run singles holidays, or those exclusively for women, gay or older travellers.

↘ Women-only mountain biking in Wales:
   www.outdoorgirlz.co.uk

↘ Red Spokes Adventure Tours take small groups of cyclists to the more remote and spectacular regions in the world, as well as running day tours in the UK:
   www.redspokes.co.uk

↘ Alpine Etape offer unique cycling holidays in the French Alps:
   www.vanillaski.com/Alpine_etape/

↘ American firm Butterfield & Robinson run seriously swish tours the world over:
   www.butterfield.com

↘ French Cycling Holidays organize exactly what you'd imagine:
   www.frenchcyclingholidays.com

↘ Italy Bike Hotels run bicycle-friendly inns across Italy, and provide route maps, safe cycle storage, maintenance help and much more:
   www.italybikehotels.it/en/

CYCLING WHILE ON HOLIDAY

An increasing number of cities worldwide are introducing bike-rental schemes which allow locals and tourists to pick up cheap communal bikes from points all around town. At the time of writing, Boris Johnson, London's pedalling mayor, planned to launch London's scheme in summer 2010. This, so Johnson promised, will offer 6,000 bicycles for hire from 400 docking stations with 10,000 docking points. It's a brave move. When a similar scheme was attempted in Cambridge in 1993, the overwhelming majority of the fleet of 300 bicycles were stolen, and the programme was abandoned.

MONTREAL

The London scheme is modelled most closely on the Bixi system, which launched in Montreal, Canada, in spring 2009. Bixi (from bicycle and taxi) started by offering 2,400 bikes at 300 stations in the city, allowing paid-up members to pick up a bicycle from a self-service station on the street and return it to any one of the other stations in the city. The first half-hour is free. Canada is an increasingly cycle-friendly country, incidentally. In the oil-rich province of Alberta, drivers who scrap cars made in 1995 or earlier are offered up to CAN$490 (£275) to replace their vehicles with a bicycle.

www.montreal.bixi.com

STOCKHOLM CITY BIKES

To hire a City Bike in Sweden, you need to buy a bike card, which are on sale on the website below or at the tourist-information office. There are two types: a season card for locals and a three-day card for tourists, which costs 125 kroner (£10.60 at the time of writing). You can only hire a bike between 6 a.m. and 6 p.m.

between April and October, but you can keep it until 9 p.m. If you keep a bike for longer than three hours on three occasions or more, or ever hang on to it for five hours, your card will be blocked.

www.citybikes.se/en/

PARIS VÉLIB'

Paris's Vélib' rental scheme is the largest system of its kind in the world, offering 20,000 bicycles at 1,450 stations throughout the city centre, roughly one station every 300 metres. You need a credit card to rent a bike, but it costs just €1 per day, provided you don't keep the bike for longer than half an hour at a time. Steep penalties are incurred if you hog a bike too long.

www.en.velib.paris.fr/

COPENHAGEN CITY BIKES

Perhaps the simplest bike-rental scheme of all exists in the legendarily bicycle-friendly Danish

capital. All you need is a 20 DKK (£2.35) coin, which you feed into a slot at one of the 110 City Bike-racks, and you're off. When you return the bike, you get your coin back.
www.bycyklen.dk/english/thecitybikeand copenhagen.aspx

There are also schemes running in other cities in the world, including Vienna (City-bike), Munich and Berlin (Call a Bike), Helsinki (Cityräder), Lyon (Vélo'v), Barcelona (Bicing), Seville (Sevici), Kraków (BikeOne), Milan (Bike-Mi), Washington DC (SmartBike) and Brussels (Villo!).

Most cities and holiday destinations have bike-hire rental firms offering bikes for an afternoon, day or more. Before you pay a deposit, make sure you know exactly what costs you will incur if the bike gets stolen or damaged, and agree with the shop any prior problems with the bike. Sometimes you are liable for far more than the bike could possibly be worth. You usually have to take whichever bike they offer you, but don't be shy to ask for an alternative if the one they offer doesn't fit or has seen better days.

CYCLING FOR SPORT AND FITNESS

You've mastered the commute, you've been on a cycling holiday – how about you have a go at cycling for sport? For some people, of course, cycling is sport. For these Lycra-clad speed demons, a bicycle is not merely a way of getting from A to B in an agreeable manner, but a piece of competitive equipment which must be tested to the max on every outing, whether heading to the post office or all the way to John O'Groats.

But just because you're not the type to see every journey as a potential time trial doesn't mean you shouldn't have a crack at cycling for sport. Though it might seem a rather intimidating prospect, there are an increasing number of events and activities catering for ordinary folk who want to take their bike to the next level and increase their fitness while they're at it. There is something for everyone, whether you fancy off-roading, cycling long distances or simply going round and round as fast as you can.

Perhaps you want to raise some money for charity by doing a sponsored ride; maybe you just want to lose a bit of flab without hitting the gym. A lot of people cycle simply because it's a way of getting fit that doesn't involve exercising in an airless room on equipment laced with the sweat of a hundred others. The marvellous thing about cycling is that you get to burn calories in a lovely setting – races and sportives take place in some of the most picturesque parts of the country, around lochs, across moors and over stunning hills. While your bottom is firming up, you'll be breathing in fresh country air and admiring a view, rather than watching CNN on mute at the gym.

Cyclists tend to be a sociable bunch, too. If you join a cycling club you can be sure that there will always be someone to gee you up if you get tired, or to hand you a Jaffa cake if you're flagging – not to mention help you should you get a puncture. No one ever gets left behind. Don't worry that everyone else will be better than you. Chances are, they won't. You'll be surprised at the range of ages and abilities, particularly on charity rides. And even if you are the one bringing up the rear, does it really matter? It's got to be better than sitting indoors getting fat in front of the telly.

SPORTIVES

If you're not the combative type but want to push yourself a bit, investigate the world of the sportive. Sportive is a slightly poncy way of describing a semi-competitive cycling challenge. It's not officially a race, but a mass participatory event involving a lot of people pedalling rather a long way – generally, but not always – as fast as they can. Some take place on closed roads; others compete with ordinary traffic.

Sportives attract bikers of all abilities, from semi-professional cyclists to wobbly newbies on a weight-loss challenge. Before I entered my first one, the 81-mile Etape Caledonia in Scotland, I was terrified that I would be at the back of the field on a bike everyone else would laugh at. But all human life was there – I saw rickety old racers ridden by even more rickety riders, and far more paunches than six-packs. The winner finished many hours ahead of the last rider to cross the line. Though the event went belly up when some lunatic decided to sabotage it by sprinkling carpet tacks along the route (ostensibly a protest against roads being closed for a few hours), I finished it in five hours, exhausted but tremendously proud of having cycled further and faster than I had ever gone before.

Many sportives, such as the Ride It! series sponsored by the UK bike chain Evans Cycles (http://www.evanscycles.com/ride-it), include a number of distance options for each event – the 'fun' rides are generally just 12 miles or so and suitable for families, a 'short' ride might be 30 miles, 'medium' 60 miles and 'long' 100 miles.

Some of the toughest sportives follow the exact routes taken by professional bike races. In the most famous sportive of all, the Etape du Tour, you can even cycle a real leg of the Tour de France a day or so before the professionals roll into town. Amateurs can also ride the legendary cobbled route of the Paris–Roubaix race, as well as the 300km Milan–San Remo slog. As the Olympic cyclist Nicole Cooke says in her book *Cycle For Life*, 'how many humble Sunday footballers can play in the world's famous stadiums, running on the same pitch as legends like Pele or Beckham or Zidane? You can't just stroll up to Wimbledon or Flushing Meadows and play on the centre court and dream of being Martina Navratilova. But cyclists can ride the Ventoux and Alpe D'Huez.'

Folding-bike owners even have their own sportives. The Brompton World Championship takes place every year and has delightfully idiosyncratic rules. A blazer or suit jacket, collared shirt and tie are compulsory. Sports attire is banned, unless it is hidden by the approved kit, and there is a prize for the best-dressed. For details, see:
www.brompton.co.uk

Another sportive with a difference is La Médocaine, an annual cycling race around the vineyards of Bordeaux. Every year, the ride, subtitled Velo Tout Vigne (Cycle Through Vines), attracts over 6,000 two-wheeled wine enthusiasts from all over France, many in fancy dress. Seven different circuits are on offer, which range from a gentle 20km route right up to a tough 80km course. Racing to the finish line is frowned upon: the real aim of the day is to enjoy as much fine wine as possible en route. Each year, local châteaux donate over 6,000 litres of wine for tastings:
www.medocainevtt.com (in French).

Sportives generally cost upwards of £10 to enter, with many charging considerably more. This fee should ensure a safe, well-signposted and marshalled route, dotted with feeding and drinking stations. You'll probably get a medal or a T-shirt at the end too, and at the bigger events you are given a timing chip to record how long it took you to reach the finish. The most popular sportives sell out months in advance; others allow riders to enter on the day. The more casual ones have a very relaxed start time, with riders asked to set off any time they like between, say, 7 a.m. and 10 a.m. Others are much more strict and allocate each rider a wave (start group), which set off every few minutes.

Some sportives have a time limit. In the strictest events, such as the Etape du Tour, failure to meet the limit will result in you being 'broomed' – your number torn off, your bike slung in the 'broom wagon' and you forced to sit on a bus, dejected and depressed, following the route at a painfully slow speed. But most of the time, if you are too slow, you will simply find that you will not have your time recorded at the end and will probably have to compete at your own risk, possibly on re-opened roads.

Cyclosport keeps a comprehensive calendar of sportives in the UK and beyond, graded by difficulty:
www.cyclosport.org

Sports Tours International organizes holiday packages to big sportives around the world, including the Etape du Tour:
www.sportstoursinternational.co.uk

FAMOUS SPORTIVES

L'ETAPE DU TOUR, FRANCE

The granddaddy of them all takes place in July each year and follows one of the notorious mountain stages of the Tour de France. Expect ludicrous gradients, mad temperatures, crazy distances and an incredible atmosphere – the roads will be closed, and the spectators out in force in preparation for the real tour, which rolls into town a day or so later. Those not resident in France can only enter via a number of specially appointed tour companies, who force you to buy into a whole package.
www.letapedutour.com

THE FRED WHITTON CHALLENGE, LAKE DISTRICT

This super-hilly 112-mile ride around the English Lake District takes in six of the major passes, including the brutal Hardknott and Wrynose.
www.fredwhittonchallenge.org.uk

THE DRAGON RIDE, WALES

This tough course in the hills and valleys of South Wales takes a circular route of either 120 or 190km and is often ridden by experienced cyclists gearing up for the Etape du Tour a few weeks later.
www.dragonride.co.uk

THE ETAPE CALEDONIA

The only closed-road sportive in the UK covers 81 miles of stunning Perthshire countryside.
www.etapecaledonia.co.uk

THE TOUR DE L'ÎLE, CANADA

Around 30,000 people do this 52km easy bike ride around Montreal every year.
www.velo.qc.ca/english/

CHARITY RIDES

Taking part in a charity ride is a great way to get fit and do some good. Many sportives are also charity events – the British Heart Foundation (www.bhf.org. uk) organizes some of the biggest rides in the UK, from the annual London to Brighton to a number of jaunts from London to Paris, including one specifically for riders on folding bikes. There are women-only rides for breast cancer, easy rides for all the family, as well as serious challenges for more experienced riders. Many charities also increasingly offer cycling adventure holidays, where participants are asked to raise a few thousand pounds in sponsorship before departure. The company Charity Challenge arranges cycling trips in the Andes, Cuba, along the Great Wall of China and beyond. www.charitychallenge.com

The pace of charity rides is often slower than pure sportives, with some participants wearing fancy dress and stopping for booze or food along the way. If you feel awkward asking your mates to sponsor you when they know full well you are mostly doing it for fun, seek out the rides where some of the entry fee goes to charity, so that even if you don't raise sponsorship you are still doing something vaguely altruistic. Beware, though, that some charities initially charge an entry fee of £50 or so and then, just as you're filling in the entry form, ask you to raise a minimum amount in sponsorship as well. They won't hold you to it usually, but you might feel a bit guilty ignoring their plea.

Some events sell out really quickly. The London to Brighton attracts 27,000 cyclists and all places are snapped up within days of going on sale.

Make sure that you are fit enough to cover the distance and, if possible, practise riding with other people beforehand. If you're only used to toddling along on your own, it can be quite a shock suddenly riding as part of a peloton.

COMPETITIVE CYCLING

British Cycling, the national governing body for cycling in the UK, is the starting point for all forms of professional bike racing, as well as grassroots competition. The organization recently overhauled its website (www.britishcycling.org.uk) and has all the information about every kind of cycle sport, including how to find your nearest club.

TRIATHLONS

This multi-event sport combines swimming, cycling and running (in that order) and is often derided as being something for people who aren't especially good at anything but OK at everything. That's true to an extent. But it is my theory that triathlons generally favour cyclists over swimmers or runners, as it tends to be the cycling leg where competitors can make up the most time. The first triathlon I ever did, in the Cotswolds, began very badly when I panicked on the open-water swim, and had to do breast stroke the whole way with my head above the water like an old lady who didn't want to get her perm wet. Once I was on my bike, however, I was soon overtaking far better swimmers, and wound up with a much more respectable time overall.

Triathlons run over all sorts of distances, from 'super sprint' events, which might involve a 400m swim, 20k bike ride and a 5km run, right up to the barely believable Iron Man, which entails a 2.4 mile (3.86km) swim, 112 mile (180km) bike ride and a 26.2 mile (42km) marathon at the end.

Triathlons are very friendly events, and often take place in some beautiful places. One of the most famous races in the UK is staged in Windsor, and includes a swim in the river near the Queen's castle. The world's biggest competition is the annual London Triathlon, which sees more than 11,000 people compete over two days. The smallest one I have ever done was in the East Yorkshire town of Goole. The river used for the swimming leg was so narrow that each of the fifty competitors had to set off individually.

Beware: it is very easy to get hooked, and this is an expensive hobby. As well as the entry fee, which is rarely less than £30, many swims take place in open water and wetsuits are mandatory – even hiring one for a weekend costs around £40. And though you can use your ordinary bike, you'll probably start hankering after some tri-bars to fix to the front to make you more aerodynamic. Then you've got all-in-one tri-suits to consider, and two different types of footwear, then a special belt to fix your number on and so it begins. No wonder triathlons tend to be dominated by the high-earning middle classes.

The British Triathlon Federation keeps a calendar of all of its accredited events: **www.britishtriathlon.org**

CYCLO-CROSS

If you're looking for something to keep you riding through the winter, you could try Cyclo-Cross, which combines cross-country running and cycling. The races are short, usually no more than an hour in length, and tend to take place on grassy courses in public parks or on school playing fields.

You don't necessarily need a special Cyclo-Cross bike to take part, but you'll need knobbly tyres to cope with off-roading. Mountain bikes are welcome at most races, and the non-technical nature of the courses means that almost anyone can take part and enjoy a race. Whatever your bike, it shouldn't be too heavy, as it'll be slung over your shoulder for some of the race as you climb over obstacles.

Local races have a relaxed, informal atmosphere, and entries are usually accepted on the day. There are often separate races for younger riders, usually with a reduced entry fee or no entry fee at all. For older riders and women, races are often shorter. Even senior races rarely last more than an hour, so taking part doesn't require a mammoth training commitment.

Search for your nearest Cyclo-Cross club on the British Cycling website: **www.britishcycling.org.uk**

CYCLE SPEEDWAY

Just like its better known motorbike cousin, cycle speedway is a form of fast and furious bike racing. It takes place on short oval dirt tracks, usually outdoors, typically 70–90 metres long. Not dissimilar, grass-track racing is making a comeback as a summer sport. Unlike other bike events, physical contact is both legal and often necessary. Four riders contest a race, usually in pairs from opposing clubs. Each match normally consists of between sixteen and twenty races.

Cycle Speedway bikes are as simple as BMX or track bikes – there are no gears, brakes, brackets, quick-release fittings, etc. Frames are often converted from mountain bikes. It's a contact sport, so many riders wear additional protection such as knee, elbow and hip pads.

Most clubs welcome newcomers, and many of them have bikes available to loan to beginners and coaches willing to tutor the basic skills. The sport is administered by British Cycling – details on their website.

Welcome to the velodrome

If you enjoyed watching Britain's track cyclists pedal to victory at the 2008 Olympics but never really understood what on earth was going on, book yourself in for a taster session at your nearest velodrome.

Despite the resurgence in cycling, velodromes – indoor or outdoor arenas containing steeply banked, ovular tracks – remain a rare breed. There are three indoor velodromes in the UK, in Manchester, Newport (south Wales) and Calshot (near Southampton), as well as twenty or so outdoor tracks. London will have a new indoor velodrome in time for the 2012 Olympics. Most are very friendly places run by enthusiastic and evangelical volunteers who, for a small fee, will be happy to introduce you to the dark arts of track cycling.

There is quite a big eek-factor cycling around a velodrome for the first time, as I discovered when I went for an induction session at the UK's oldest arena in Herne Hill, south London. The outdoor track has an illustrious history – it's the only finals venue from the 1948 and 1908 London Olympics still in active use and was where the Olympic and Tour de France star Bradley Wiggins got his first taste for the sport.

The first scary thing is not having any brakes. The logic is that no rider should be able to stop or slow down quicker than their rivals. Plus, with everyone going in the same direction and no reckless delivery truck likely to suddenly lurch around the corner, they are unnecessary. Having no brakes also makes the bikes as lightweight and aerodynamic as possible. I am used to cycling with my hands covering my brakes just in case so to ride without them felt foolhardy in the extreme. How on earth would I stop?

Only track bikes with fixed wheels are allowed to ride the velodrome, so if you don't have a true fixie (see chapter 1, p. 36), you'll have to borrow one. At Herne Hill, rental of a bike and helmet is included in the very reasonable £4 induction fee.

Twenty or so other novices joined my induction session – all men, alas, as despite the stunning performance by Rebecca Romero, Victoria Pendleton and the other fine women cyclists on Team GB, track cycling is a resolutely male-dominated sport. Under the instruction of some eccentric but encouraging coaches (one a national Masters champion), we were taught how to stop by controlling the spin of the pedals. Track bikes have no freewheel, so whenever the wheels move, so do the pedals. To speed up or slow down, you apply different pressure to the pedals. If you try to freewheel, prepare yourself to come down to earth (and the bottom of the banking) with a nasty bump. There are no gears either, so if you want to speed up, pedal harder.

The other skill you need to learn is how to cycle in a pack. Pro track cyclists keep just millimetres apart in order to benefit from the slipstream of the riders ahead; at Herne Hill, we were told to aim to keep within a bike's length of the rider ahead. This is deeply daunting, especially when the bloke in front has never ridden a track bike either. For the first few laps, I swore under my breath and grasped the handlebars like a shipwreck victim clutching the last bit of wreckage. I'm not sure I blinked the whole way round.

Quickly, though, things started falling into place. I found a rhythm, and some courage, and suddenly I was doing it. We rode as a pack, taking it in turns to ride at the front for half a lap, before going up the banking and to the back of the group. Ride at the front for much more and you get absolutely shattered, because you are riding right into the wind while sheltering your comrades, so you do your turn then slip to the back.

Track racing has many different formats – points races, scratch races, handicaps, sprints, the Madison, the Keirin – each with their own rules and tactics. I contented myself with simply going round and round in endless circles. It was quite enough for one morning.

MOUNTAIN-BIKE RACING

DOWNHILL

If you like hurtling down mountains, flying over jumps and bumps and tearing around tight corners, you'll love downhill racing. Riders race individually against the clock on a course which is predominantly downhill – often dropping between 300 and 600 metres in perhaps 2.5 km of racing. Races usually last between two and five minutes and specialist kit is recommended, if not required – think a full-face helmet and body armour. You'll need a downhill mountain bike too, with loads of suspension, broad knobbly tyres, a strong, light frame and very good brakes.

FOUR CROSS (4X)

A contest between four riders who compete against each other over a short, mainly downhill course including jumps, bumps and terrifying corners. First over the line wins, and events usually involve a series of qualifying rounds or 'motos', and then semis and finals. The start is controlled by a BMX-style mechanical gate. You need a special mountain bike – a 'hardtail' model with no rear suspension – and as much protective gear as possible.

CROSS-COUNTRY

These races take place on a marked lap (typically 3–6km) with climbing, descending, single-track and technical sections with tight turns, narrow tracks, rocks, mud or other difficult terrain.

CYCLING TO GET FIT [AND A BETTER BODY]

You don't have to compete to cycle for fitness. Often just biking to work instead of taking the bus is enough to improve your health, especially if you were a rather sedentary person in a past life. According to the British Heart Foundation, cycling at least 20 miles per week reduces the risk of coronary heart disease to less than half that for non-cyclists. Curmudgeonly tycoon Alan Sugar told the *Daily Mail* in 2009 that he had lost three stone by taking twice-weekly bike rides around the Essex countryside – so pleased was Surallun with his new svelte figure that he even allowed himself to be photographed in head-to-toe orange and blue Lycra, an image I've never quite managed to erase from my memory.

Cycling for 8 miles at 12mph is equivalent to:

- **30 minutes of football or squash**
- **50 minutes of tennis**
- **2.5 miles of brisk walking**
- **24 holes of golf ***

If you are overweight, get a check-up from your GP before you start, and go for long and easy rides rather than going flat out in high gears until you're ready to burst. As you get fitter, your aerobic fitness will increase and your heart will get stronger. If you keep track of your resting heart rate using a heart-rate monitor, you will see it gradually drop. Professional cyclists have crazily low resting rates – the heart of Miguel Indurain, the legendary Spanish rider, used to beat just 28 times a minute. The average heart rate is usually about 70–75 beats per minute.

---

* From Dr Ronald Williams, *On Your Bike*, 'Cycling and Health'

Calorie comparison

Calculated for a 10-stone person doing 30 minutes of exercise:

- ↘ Moderate cycling at 10–11.9mph: *191 calories*
- ↘ Vigorous cycling at 14–15.9mph: *318 calories*
- ↘ Running at 7mph: *365 calories*
- ↘ Football: *286 calories*
- ↘ Jogging: *222 calories*

- ↘ Aerobics: *206 calories*
- ↘ Badminton: *143 calories*
- ↘ Fast ballroom dancing: *143 calories*
- ↘ Golf: *143 calories*
- ↘ Gardening: *127 calories*
- ↘ Sleeping: *29 calories*

Calculated using the activity calculator on www.caloriesperhour.com

Cycling regularly will also give you a great body – a great lower body, at least (cyclists tend to have very weedy arms, alas). Cycling burns fat, increases muscle tone in the legs, the calves in particular, and strengthens the heart and lungs. It is far lower impact than running, so you are less likely to hurt yourself. The only minor downer is that, because it is non weight-bearing, it won't do anything to keep your bones strong.

Cycle regularly, and you will soon notice a change in your legs and bottom. Sometimes women worry they will end up with thunder thighs like Chris Hoy. Panic not: to get Hoy-like hamhocks, you need freakish DNA and an Olympic training regime. It is true, however, that cycling tends not to make legs thinner, but it will certainly make them more toned and shapely. Women's magazines often like to pretend cycling will banish cellulite. I can sadly attest that this is nonsense, though it will firm up your bum massively. When Olympic gold medallist Victoria Pendleton stripped off for FHM in 2009, she told the men's mag how proud she was of her legs – 'they don't wobble, they're not cellulite-y,' she said, before admitting that, to keep them that way, she spends up to six hours a day in the gym.

DIET

Don't. Being able to eat what you like is one of the joys of cycling. I have been known to polish off several Double Deckers on a long ride. Carbohydrate-loading before a big excursion works for me – a big bowl of pasta the night before and then lots of porridge and toast for breakfast, though 'serious' cyclists tend to pooh-pooh carb loading, favouring a mix of protein and carbs plus plenty of nutrient-rich fruit and veg. Professional cyclists have neurotic eating habits, counting out the exact number of pasta shapes and measuring their rice to the milligram. Poor old them. The rest of us should enjoy our food as much as the cycling.

CYCLING INDOORS

If you don't have the time, weather or daylight hours always to take your bike into the great outdoors, there are a number of indoor options.

Spinning

The thought of being stuck in a sweaty room full of people on exercise bikes with music blaring, lights flashing and an instructor shouting doesn't really appeal to me, but you may beg to differ. Spinning classes last 45 minutes to an hour and take participants through routines that are designed to simulate terrain and situations similar to riding a bike outdoors. Some of the movements and positions include hill climbs, sprints and interval training.

Turbo trainer

This contraption consists of a stand and resistance unit to which you attach your rear wheel. More expensive turbo trainers allow you to vary the resistance to mimic hills; others are fixed on the one level. Some turbo trainers are a real faff because they require you to take out your quick-release skewer and replace it with the one included with your trainer. For this reason, some people keep a spare back wheel permanently hooked up. Using a turbo trainer isn't rocket science – you basically just pedal – but it is very, very boring, and unbelievably sweaty, and you will probably need a heart-rate monitor to give your sessions some structure. Without the natural air resistance to cool you down, you'll soon be sweating cobs, so invest in a fan or use the machine in the garage or garden. The fanciest turbo trainers link up with GPS-enabled bike computers, and can recreate a real ride, varying gradients at appropriate times.

Roller racing

Roller racing was once a popular sport in the UK, and huge crowds would gather in ballrooms, cinemas and hotels to see the cyclists race on roller rigs. Rollers make it possible to ride indoors without moving forwards, like a turbo trainer but without any resistance. Since 2000, the Rollapaluza crew have been leading the resurgence, organizing races in nightclubs and pubs up and down the country.
www.rollapaluza.com

STRETCHING AFTER CYCLING

I never stretch after cycling, preferring either to make a cup of tea or collapse in a heap, depending on how far I have gone, but some people really feel the benefit. Here are a few exercises for stretching the major muscle groups taxed by cycling.

Glutes (bottom)

Lie on your back with your knees bent and your feet flat on the floor. Place your right ankle on your left thigh, just above the knee, and pull your legs towards your tummy until you feel a stretch on the outside of your right bum cheek. Repeat on the other side.

Calves

Find some stairs, ideally with a railing or other object you can hold on to for balance, if needed. Stand on the step with your heel and arch hanging off the back of the step; keep just the ball of your foot and toes on the step. Raise up on your toes as high as you can in a slow and controlled manner. Pause for a second at the top.

Quads (front of your thighs)

Stand on your right leg and grab on to your left ankle with your left hand. Hold on to something or someone for balance with your other hand if you need to. Standing straight, pull your left foot gently up towards your bottom so that your knee bends and you feel the stretch down the front of your thigh. Hold and repeat with the other leg.

Hamstrings

Bend over at the waist and place one foot forwards with the heel on the floor and the toe pointing upwards. The other foot should be placed directly behind, flat on the floor. Lower the body slightly with the weight on the front foot, which is where the hamstring stretch should be felt. Repeat with the other leg.

OCCUPATIONAL HAZARDS OF BEING A CYCLIST

SADDLE SORES

Sore muscles aren't the only way your body can suffer for your cycling habit. Spend too long in the saddle and you could develop saddle sores, an unpleasant medical condition usually caused by extended pressure and friction combined with lax hygiene. They are usually a form of skin infection in a form similar to a boil or pimple, but severe ones can be open sores. Real saddle sores can be painful in the extreme, and require treatment with special cream and, ideally, a few days off the bike. The key to avoiding them is good hygiene: never wear bike shorts more than once and start every ride squeaky clean.

Avoiding saddle sores and sore bottom syndrome (SBS)

Some people are more prone to SBS than others. If you are overweight, you are far more likely to suffer, though I know plenty of skinnies who are always moaning every time we go for a ride.

To stave off SBS, get out of the saddle at regular intervals throughout the ride to give your bottom a rest. You can also experiment with your saddle height and angle, tilting it backwards or forwards or up or down and see if that helps. If chafing seems to be the problem, grease up before a ride using Vaseline or an anti-bacterial chamois cream, and perhaps try wearing a different sort of underwear. Sometimes wearing ordinary knickers or boxers underneath padded cycling shorts can be a problem. If all else fails, you could always buy a new saddle or – even more extreme – you could buy a different style of bike. Recumbents distribute body weight very differently to ordinary bikes and are far kinder to bottoms.

LOWER BACK PAIN

A very common ailment among the two-wheeled fraternity, which can be avoided by keeping your leg muscles 'long' and improving your flexibility. Sit on the floor with your legs straight in front of you, and bend forward from the waist as far as you can go. Go as far as you can, ideally touching your toes, and hold the stretch.

CYCLING FOR PEOPLE WITH KNEE PROBLEMS

If you have problems with your knees, you need to take extra precautions when cycling, which can exacerbate or trigger various issues. First of all, make sure your saddle is the right height – too low and your knee will be too bent; too high and you'll overstretch. Maladjusted cleats can also be a problem if you ride with clipless pedals. You want them to allow your feet to be at their natural angle, and to move about a little bit. Look for cleats offering 'float'.

Most people get sore knees if they cycle for a long time at too high a gear, so be sure to give your knees a rest with easy gears every now and again.

The best way to prevent knee problems is to do core stability exercises, or pilates or yoga. I find all three incredibly tedious, but on the rare occasions I stick at them for a reasonable length of time, I really notice a difference.

I heartily recommend getting hold of a stability roller. These sausage-shaped foam rolls cost around a tenner and can be used for stretching, massage, stability exercises, core strengthening, sports injury, rehabilitation, physiotherapy, pilates and yoga. Do a bit of Googling and you can pick one up cheaply, and find lots of exercises that really do make a difference.

Cycling hero: Annie Londonderry

Whenever someone tries to claim that you can't really cycle in a skirt, I tell them about Annie Londonderry, the audacious Boston housewife who, in the late nineteenth century, abandoned her husband and children to become the first woman to circumnavigate the globe on a bicycle.

When Annie pedalled away on 25 June 1894, she was dressed in full Victorian regalia – floor length funereal skirt, puff-sleeved tailored jacket over a crisp white shirt and bow tie and a very jaunty brimmed hat. All she carried with her, according to her great-grandnephew Peter Zheutlin, who wrote her biography, is 'a revolver, a change of underwear and a dream of freedom'. She was also riding a bicycle – a 42-pound clunker – for the very first time.

Annie was what can only be described as 'a bit of a one'. An ace self-publicist, she claimed she was embarking on her international adventure to settle a wager between two wealthy Boston sugar merchants. 'I am to go around the earth in fifteen months, returning with five thousand dollars, and starting only with the clothes on my back,' she declared at the press conference she held to announce her adventure.

By the time she reached Chicago in the September, Annie was thoroughly hacked off with her cumbersome attire. She briefly toyed with jacking it all in, before blagging herself a much lighter men's bike and donning a pair of bloomers, which she later claimed were such a hit with the gentlemen she met en route that she received 'no less than two hundred proposals of marriage'. Though her outfit change shows that shorts are best for a really long ride, she is proof that you can still manage a good 1,000 miles in a skirt.

It is still not entirely clear how much of her route Annie actually cycled – there is certainly evidence she hopped on a fair few trains and ferries along the way. But her chutzpah, determination and all round sartorial daring are an inspiration to us all.

Cycling hero: Beryl Burton MBE

Though bike racing remains a tiresomely male-dominated sport, many of Britain's most successful cyclists are women, including BMX star Shanaze Reade, world champion road racer Nicole Cooke and Olympic track maestros Victoria Pendleton and Rebecca Romero.

But long before these athletes entered the world's consciousness at the 2008 Beijing Olympics, there was Beryl Burton, a Leeds lass who many consider the greatest female cyclist of all time.

After getting married in 1957 aged just seventeen, Beryl threw herself into competitive cycling with her husband Charlie as her coach and mentor. Despite technological advances, no woman has ever broken one of her records – in 1967, she rode 277.25 miles in twelve hours. Back then, no man had ever ridden the time trial so fast, and she smashed the previous record by almost six miles. Legend has it that as she passed the leading man she offered him a stick of liquorice – 'the poor dear seemed to be struggling a bit.'

She passed on the cycling genes to her daughter Denise, who also went on to become a professional cyclist. Beryl cycled throughout her pregnancy, only giving up the day 'the bump stopped me from squeezing behind the handlebars'. She only had one motto: 'Miles – plenty of 'em!'

Mother and daughter were both selected to represent Great Britain in the 1972 world championship, and ten years later the pair set a British 10-mile record for women riding a tandem bicycle: 21 minutes, 25 seconds. In 1984, Beryl applied to compete in the inaugural Women's Tour de France, but was knocked back – not because of her age (she was forty-seven by then) but because she didn't have any road-racing qualifications for that year. She could have competed in the end, after another rider dropped out, but her Yorkshire pride stopped her from accepting a place after the initial rejection.

She died of heart failure during a training ride shortly before her fifty-ninth birthday, but her memory lives on in the Beryl Burton Cycle Way, which connects Harrogate and Knaresborough, and in a memorial garden in her hometown of Morley.

GLOSSARY

ALLEN KEY: Simple hexagonal-ended tool used to adjust many bits of a bicycle. Often come as a set or as part of a multi-tool device.

ALLEYCAT: A scavenger-hunt-type race where riders have to go to checkpoints across the city as fast as they can. Popular with couriers. Illegal.

ALL THE GEAR AND NO IDEA: A rider with the best kit and no skills to make the most of it.

AUDAX: A type of long-distance cycling ride run under rules laid down by Audax UK (a cycling club), which stipulate, among other things, that participants have to make it to checkpoints by certain times. You can buy special Audax bikes, which are road bikes designed for comfort. For more info, see www.audax.uk.net

BICYCLE POLO: Urban take on a toff's sport – riders carry mallets on fixed-gear bikes to play polo in city streets and playgrounds.

BIKE SALMON: Cyclist who insists on going the wrong way up a one-way street. Coined by Bike Snob NYC.

BIKE-SHAPED OBJECT (BSO): A rubbish flatpack bike sold by non-specialist shops.

BONK: What happens if cyclists run out of energy after not eating and drinking enough on a long ride. Also known as The Wall or The Knock. Usually used as a verb, e.g. 'I totally bonked on that last 10k.'

BOSSES: Little holes on the frame used for bolting on items such as racks or bottle cages.

BOTTOM BRACKET: Rotating unit at the bottom of the bike frame that connects the cranks on either side of the bottom bracket shell to each other.

CADENCE: Pedalling rate. The faster you pedal, the higher your cadence.

CASSETTE: Collection of sprockets that fit on the rear wheel's freehub for use with derailleur gears. Also known as the 'block'.

CHAIN RING: A toothed ring attached to the crankset that drives the chain and, in turn, the sprockets and rear wheel of a bicycle.

CHAMOIS: The padding in cycling shorts. Sometimes removable; sometimes not.

CLEAT: Metal or plastic piece attached to the bottom of cycling shoes which locks the shoe and pedal together.

COASTER BRAKE: Internal hub brake operated by pedalling backwards.

CRANKSET: Or simply 'the crank' – lever arm joining the pedal to the chainwheel and bottom bracket.

CRITERIUM: A fast road race that takes place on a short circuit, usually on closed roads in a town centre.

DERAILLEUR: Most common method of gear change, whereby the chain is shifted from one sprocket (or cog or chainwheel) to the next using a derailleur mechanism. Pronounced de-rail-yur, the word comes from the French for derailment, i.e. something moving away from the track/cog (and on to the next).

DOMESTIQUE: French term for altruistic members of a racing team who support their star rider by sheltering them from the wind, fetching their water bottles, etc.

DRAFTING: Cycling directly behind someone and taking advantage of their slipstream.

DRIVETRAIN: The collective name for the chainset, chain and sprockets that drive the bike forward by transmitting leg power into rear-wheel rotation.

DROP-OUT: U-shaped metal bracket on the end of front fork or rear stay that you slot the wheels into.

FAKENGER: A person who rides a fixed gear bike and dresses like a bike messenger/courier but isn't. Widely mocked by real couriers. Also known as Posengers.

FIXED GEAR: A system in which the pedals turn whenever the bike is moving. Sometimes called fixed wheel.

FLOAT: Cleats which have a bit of lateral movement, i.e. you can wiggle your feet from side to side a little.

FORK: Bike part that holds the front wheel and allows the rider to steer and balance.

FRANKENBIKE: A bike built from the parts of other bicycles.

FREEWHEEL: A mechanism that allows the rear wheel to rotate while the pedals aren't moving. Sometimes called the 'block'.

GRANNY GEAR: The largest chain ring and smallest cog, a very small gear for the most brutal hills. Masochistic cyclists will do everything they can to avoid using their granny gear, or even their whole granny ring.

HEADSET: The bearings within the head tube to which the forks are attached.

HEADTUBE: The frame tube through which the steerer runs.

HUB: Metal bit in the middle of a wheel which is connected to the rim by the spokes.

HUB GEAR: Variable gear contained within the rear-wheel hub.

INVISIBLE HILL: Head wind.

MECH: Bikey slang for 'mechanism', as in 'front mech', the device that pushes the chain on to a larger or smaller chain ring or sprocket.

PELOTON: French term for the main group of cyclists in a race.

PRESTA VALVE: Type of inner-tube valve common on skinny tyres.

PSI: Unit of pressure used for bicycle tyres. Stands for Pounds per Square Inch.

ROAD RASH: Grazing you get if you fall off your bike and scrape off some skin.

SADDLE SORES: Unpleasant condition on the bottom caused by a combination of friction and bacteria. Avoid with a properly adjusted saddle, impeccable hygiene and clean padded shorts.

SCHRADER VALVE: Type of valve used on some inner tubes, particularly on Dutch and mountain bikes. Fatter than a presta valve.

SEAT POST: A hollow tube that holds the saddle and slots into the seat tube.

SEAT STAY: Frame tube joining the top of the seat tube to the rear drop-out.

SPD: Shimano Pedaling Dynamics – a range of clipless pedals and matching shoes designed by the Japanese components manufacturer Shimano. Often used as a catch-all name for cycling shoes with cleats.

SPORTIVE: Long-distance, organized, mass-participation cycling challenges (not races).

SPROCKET: A gear cog on the rear cassette that is turned by the chain.

STEERER: The tube that connects the forks to the stem and handlebars.

STEM: Bit which connects the handlebars to the steerer.

TRACK PUMP: Upright bike pump, the best and most efficient way to inflate bicycle tyres.

TREAD: The middle part of a tyre that makes contact with the ground.

VELODROME: A cycling stadium with a steeply banked track.

WICKING: Property of technical fabrics which promise to transfer sweat away from the body into the open air.

FURTHER READING, WATCHING AND LISTENING

BIKE BOOKS I LIKE

The Escape Artist by Matt Seaton
(Fourth Estate, 2003)
Touching, very readable memoir from the Guardian's bike-mad Matt Seaton about the travails of balancing work, life, babies and cycling. Includes a six-page explanation of just why professional cyclists – or wannabe professional cyclists – shave their legs.

French Revolutions by Tim Moore
(Vintage, 2002)
One of the very few funny books about cycling, this is the tale of one ordinary man's attempt to complete the Tour de France. Moore, a self-confessed layabout, prepares for the 2,256-mile test of masochism with one spinning class and sets off to do battle with French bureaucracy, his own body and the dreaded Mont Ventoux.

Boy Racer by Mark Cavendish
(Ebury Press, 2008)
Sweary but illuminating autobiography by Britain's greatest Tour de France cyclist, who, aged just twenty-three, won four stages at the Grande Boucle in 2008. Manx man Cavendish doesn't pussyfoot around, slags off a good chunk of the pro-cycling world, reveals an addiction to Walkers Sensations crisps and explains why he never showers before a big race (ew).

In Pursuit of Glory by Bradley Wiggins
(Orion, 2008)
This autobiography of the young Olympic cyclist with the silly haircut is unremarkable except for his description of what happened after he won gold at the 2004 Olympics. Unable to cope with the comedown, Wiggins switched the velodrome for the local pub, where he would regularly drink twelve pints and return home to his pregnant wife. Incredibly, he still managed to nab two more golds at Beijing in 2008 – proof beer and cycling aren't enemies after all. I'll drink to that.

It's Not about the Bike by Lance Armstrong
(Yellow Jersey Press, 2001)
Some people can't stomach the arrogance of the seven-time Tour de France winner, but this book, in which the Texan explains how he fought back from the testicular cancer that almost killed him, is a great read. The sequel, Every Second Counts, is not nearly as good.

Around the World on Two Wheels by Peter Zheutlen (Citadel Press Books, 2007)
Enjoyable tale of the outrageous Annie Londonderry, who in 1895 became the first woman to bicycle around the world. Or at least, she claimed she had cycled the whole way – Zheutlen, a distant relative of the feisty Jewish mother-of-three, discovers that his ancestor had a little help from public transport along the way.

Cycling's Greatest Misadventures, ed. Erich Schweikher (Casagrande Press, 2007)
This anthology of real-life bicycling disaster stories is a bit of a mixed bag, but has flashes of greatness. Includes a very poignant tale of travelling across America by bike, a jolly account about an amateur beating Miguel Indurain (the legendary pro cyclist whose heart rate was so low he was barely alive), and the story of horny teenage boys who try to sabotage an all-women bike race using drawing pins.

Put Me Back on My Bike by **William Fotheringham (Yellow Jersey Press, 2007)**
Brilliant account of the rise and fall of Tom Simpson, the legendary British cyclist who died during the Tour de France, near the top of Mont Ventoux, after imbibing a fatal cocktail of speed and alcohol.

The Cyclist's Companion, ed. **George Theohari (Think Publishing, 2007)**
Perfect toilet reading, this compendium includes all manner of cycling-related nuggets, such as the record distance for cycling backwards (i.e. sitting on the handlebars facing the wrong way) for one hour (29.1km) and a list of musicians who cycle.

TECHIE BOOKS AND GUIDES

Richard's Bicycle Book by **Richard Ballantine (Pan Books, 1977)**
Possibly the most famous cycling book ever written, this no-nonsense guide to buying, maintaining and riding bikes is still one of the best. It dips in and out of print, but secondhand copies are easy to come by.

City Cycling by **Richard Ballantine (Snow Books, 2007)**
Useful, pocket-sized guide to cycling in the city from Ballantine. Ignore the dodgy photography and soak up some tips.

Cycle for Life by **Nicole Cooke (Kyle Cathie, 2008)**
Informative guide to cycling from Britain's top Olympic cyclist. Has an emphasis on cycling for sport and training, so more for people wanting to take their cycling up a gear rather than those who just want to bimble around town.

The Bike Book by **Fred Milson (Haynes Publishing, 2003)**
No-nonsense maintenance book.

The Complete Bike Book by **Chris Sidwells (Dorling Kindersley, 2005)**
Techie but comprehensive guide to cycling, with an emphasis on cycling for sport. Warning: features more Lycra than a Mr Motivator video.

Bicycle Repair Step-by-Step by **Rob Van Der Plas (Van der Plas Publications, 2003)**
Old-school guide to fixing bikes.

Cyclecraft by **John Franklin (TSO, 2007)**
Yawnsome but useful guide to safe cycling – explains in detail everything from how to navigate a gyratory system to how to ride through a ford. The book covers the whole syllabus for Bikeability, the new all-ages version of the cycling proficiency.

BIKE MAGAZINES (ON- AND OFF-LINE)

Momentum
Canadian bike culture mag with a focus on everyday cycling. PDFs available via: www.momentumplanet.com

Road.cc
This online cycling magazine is mostly about road cycling, and has good product reviews and lively forums: www.road.cc

Rouleur
Quarterly cycling magazine with moody photography and thoughtful writing. www.rouleur.cc

The Ride
Classy journal featuring superb photography and varied writing. http://www.theridejournal.com

BIKE BLOGS

Bike Hacks: *A frequently updated treasure trove of cool, interesting and useful stuff.* http://bikehacks.com/

Bike Hugger: *Pedal-pushing off-shoot of the world's biggest eco website, Tree Hugger.* http://bikehugger.com

The Bike Show: *Opinionated blog from Jack Thurston, who presents the Bike Show on Resonance FM.* http://thebikeshow.net/

Bike Snob NYC: *Acerbic social commentary from the Big Apple's biggest bike fascist.* http://bikesnobnyc.blogspot.com/

Copenhagen Cycle Chic: *The blog that spawned a movement. Celebrates the simplicity and elegance of cycling in the Danish capital.* www.copenhagencyclechic.com

Cyclotherapy: *This is the* Independent's *contribution to the biking blogosphere.* http://cyclotherapy.independentminds.livejournal.com

Guardian **bike blog:** *I'll get roasted if I don't mention this: bicycling broadsheet journalists pontificate on all things two-wheeled.* www.guardian.co.uk/environment/series/bike-blog

Huffington Post **bike culture blog:** *Left-wing American liberals blog about bikes.* www.huffingtonpost.com/news/bike-culture

London Cycle Chic: *Blog off-shoot of the Cycle Chic online boutique. Great for keeping up with the latest bike trends, particularly relating to Dutch bikes.* http://londoncyclechic.blogspot.com/

New York Times **bike blog:** *Updated a few times a week with thoughtful, if rather dry, blog posts.* http://cityroom.blogs.nytimes.com/category/spokes/

Velorution: *Bike blog run by a London bike shop, full of bike porn and strong opinions.* www.velorution.biz

USEFUL WEBSITES

Bike For All: *Handy resource which can answer pretty much all of your bicycling queries.* www.bikeforall.net

British Cycling: *The national governing body for cycle sport in the UK.* www.britishcycling.org.uk

CTC: *The website of the CTC (the Cyclists' Touring Club – a national organization for cyclists) is a mine of information on everything from safety to route planning.* www.ctc.org.uk

Forestry Commission: *The Forestry Commission's website has a good cycling section which will suggest off-road routes near a British town or forest of your choice.* www.forestry.gov.uk/cycling

Sustrans: *Sustainable transport charity responsible for the national cycle network.* www.sustrans.org.uk

FILMS

The Bicycle Film Festival is held in thirty-nine cities worldwide every year and shows films which celebrate the bike in all forms and styles.
www.bicyclefilmfestival.com

Here are my three favourite films in which bicycles have a role:

Jules et Jim

The bicycle plays a small but significant part in this 1962 Truffaut film about a ménage à trois between two friends and the gorgeous but difficult Catherine. The trio happily pedal through the French countryside during the salad days of their unconventional relationship, but three soon becomes a crowd, and when Catherine trades two wheels for four and starts zooming around in a motor car, things go horribly wrong. A coincidence? Mais non.

A Boy, a Girl and a Bike

In the sadly overlooked 1949 British film, Honor Blackman puts on high-waisted sailor shorts and a snug woollen jersey (and a woeful Yorkshire accent) to play Susie, the top totty of a mill town who spends her days weaving and her weekends bike racing. This two-wheeled goddess has no problems navigating a crossbar, and beats most of her male admirers at their own game.

Breaking Away

Coming-of-age movie set in a US university town where a group of townie friends get together to compete against the stuck-up college crowd. Stars Dennis Quaid and won an Oscar in 1979 for Best Screenplay.

SELECTED BIBLIO-GRAPHY

Ballantine, Andrew and Grant, Richard: *Richard's Ultimate Bicycle Book* (Dorling Kindersley, London: 1992)

Cycling Plus: The Bicycle Book (Weidenfeld & Nicolson: 2005)

Ennis, Philip: *Cycling – A Source Book* (Pelham Books, London: 1984)

Harrell, Julie: *A Women's Guide to Bikes & Biking* (Van der Plas Publications, San Francisco: 1999)

Liggett, Phil: *The Complete Book of Performance Cycling* (CollinsWillow, London: 1992)

Rendell, Matt: *Blazing Saddles* (Quercus, London: 2007)

Ritchie, Andrew: *King of the Road* (Wildwood House, London: 1975)

Seaton, Matt: *On Your Bike* (Black Dog Publishing, London: 2006)

Sidwells, Chris: *The Complete Bike Book* (Dorling Kindersley, London: 2005)

Whatmore, John: *The CTC Book of Cycling* (David & Charles, Newton Abbot: 1983)

Wilcockson, John: *Bicycle* (Marshall Cavendish, London: 1980)

INDEX

ACKNOWLEDGEMENTS

This book would never have happened without the wonderful Juliet Annan, my editor and cheer-leader at Penguin. This was all her idea, and it is her enthusiasm and support which kept me going through the darker days of writing about puncture repair and the best way to approach a multi-lane roundabout.

Neil Daniels is my favourite cycling companion and has put up with more hill-related tantrums and authorly anxieties than a man should really have to bear. I couldn't have done this without him and I will be forever grateful for his blunt East Yorkshire feedback and unfailing good humour during long bike rides and the even longer writing process.

Lexy Topping is a brilliant friend and astute proofreader; Dan Lerner deserves huge thanks for giving me a push up some steep hills over the years. My generous *Guardian* colleague Matt Seaton went beyond the call of duty by reading the first draft and providing enormously helpful feedback; so did Stuart Millar. The keen eyes of Lucy Hart and Ben Mears also made everything better.

Jenny Lord provided perceptive comments and has been kind and patient throughout. Mark Read's stunning photographs perfectly convey the effortless joy of cycling and I am delighted that Olivier Kugler agreed to illustrate my words. Thanks too to John Hamilton and Sarah Fraser for the inspired design and to everyone else at Penguin who has helped *Bicycle* weave its way into book shops.

Respect also due to David Dansky from Cycle Training UK, Silka Kennedy-Todd at TFL, Victoria Hazael and Chris Peck at the CTC, Jack Thurston from Resonance FM's Bike Show, Rob Ainsley from realcycling.blogspot.com, Louise Rondel, Paul Wood from the Metropolitan Police, Amy Fleuriot and Sarah Buck from Cyclodelic, Caz Nicklin from cyclechic.co.uk and Jos van Veldhoven from Tour de Ville. And to my boss, Nick Hopkins, who somehow allowed me to take a sabbatical during the school summer holidays.